Faithful

Fatherhood

Faithful

Fatherhood

Christopher Cornelius Walls

Faithful Fatherhood

Copyright © 2024 by Christopher Cornelius Walls

Published by Christopher Cornelius Walls
ISBN: 979-8-218-57329-4

This book is a work of nonfiction. The events described and the perspectives shared are based on the author's personal experiences and reflections. Any names or details may have been altered to protect the privacy of the individuals involved.

Dedication

To my beloved parents,

Reginald Anthony Walls Sr. and Valerie Marie Walls,

For your unwavering love, strength, and sacrifice. You taught me resilience, faith, and the power of family. Every word in these pages carries a piece of the love and lessons you instilled in me. Thank you for being my foundation and guiding light.

With all my heart, I dedicate this to you.

"A father's love is a fortress, built brick by brick through sacrifice, strength, and unwavering faith. He stands tall through storms, a shelter against the harshest winds, embodying grace and endurance. His heart beats with the silent promise to guard, guide, and give, even when the path is difficult and uncertain. For in his faithfulness, he reflects the truest image of love—one that does not falter, even in the face of trials. Through him, we learn that fatherhood is not just a role, but a calling, a legacy of courage and compassion that lives on."

Christopher Cornelius Walls

Table of Contents

Table of Contents (Continued)

Table of Contents (Continued)

For Kenyon: My Brother, My Best Friend

I would like to take a moment to honor my brother, Kenyon Walls, whose untimely passing occurred during the finalization of this book. Though he is not part of the story itself, he is forever etched in my heart as a brother and a best friend.

Kenyon and I shared countless conversations—long talks filled with laughter, reflection, and encouragement. His words always uplifted me, and his unwavering belief in me was a source of strength.

His words carried a weight of love and reverence that I will hold onto forever. Though my heart is heavy with sadness that he will not see many more days with me, I am profoundly grateful for the time we had and for the gift of having him as my brother.

This book is dedicated, in part, to his memory, and I hope that through my words, his love and belief in me shine through. Thank you, Kenyon, for everything.

Acknowledgements

To my family, and friends—thank you for being the constants in my life, the shoulders to lean on, and the hearts that have shared in my joys and sorrows. Your unwavering love and support have carried me through life's challenges and victories, shaping the man I am today.

You've been a part of the memories that fill these pages—whether through laughter, tears, or lessons learned along the way. I am grateful for the roles each of you has played in my journey. This book is as much a testament to your influence as it is to my experiences. Thank you for walking this road with me, for believing in me, and for being part of my story.

With love and gratitude,

Christopher Cornelius Walls

Prologue Life Today

Life didn't turn out the way I envisioned it years ago, but somehow, in its unpredictability, it has taken a shape I can live with—one built on resilience, love, and a shared history of survival. My two sons, now ten and twelve years old, have evolved in ways that still astonish me. They aren't the same scared, broken little boys who arrived at my doorstep years ago, clutching remnants of innocence in their tiny hands. They've grown, matured, and learned to carry the weight of their experiences with a quiet, unimaginable strength. Their laughter is no longer a thin veil masking fear; it's the sound of healing, the sound of a childhood reclaimed. When they laugh now, I feel something inside me heal, too.

My nephew, now eighteen years old, stands at the crossroads of adulthood. Watching him grow has been like witnessing a flower bloom in rocky soil. He was never supposed to carry the burdens life threw at him—no one that young should—but he did, and with a grace that humbled me. He's been tested by life's cruelest winds, and yet here he is, unbowed, wiser for it. Now, as he stands on the edge of his future, I don't just see the boy I helped raise; I see a man who's faced the flames and emerged not unscathed, but stronger. He carries himself with the kind of quiet dignity that can only be forged through trial and perseverance.

The home we live in today isn't just four walls and a roof—it's a fortress of love and survival. Every smile that spreads across my sons' faces, every joke they share, every moment of peace in our home feels like a victory that was hard-fought and hard-won. There's a quiet contentment now, a knowing that no matter what challenges life hurls at us next, we will face them together, bound by the unbreakable ties we've forged through fire.

But to fully understand where we are today, you need to understand where we've been. You need to walk with us through the chaos, the unbearable moments of panic, the hopeless breakdowns that no one saw, and the relentless hope that somehow—despite all odds—kept us moving forward when giving up felt like the only option. Ours is not just a story of survival; it is a story of love. The kind of love that refuses to give up, the kind of love that digs in its heels and holds on when the world gives you every reason to let go.

Chapter 1

A Christmas Miracle – The Last Child

"Come on, push! She's going to beat us!"

If you've ever wondered what it feels like to be born under pressure, I'm probably one of the few people who can tell you firsthand. My entrance into this world was less like a gentle lullaby and more like the final lap of a high-stakes race. But we weren't racing just any clock that Christmas morning in 1985. We were racing against another baby, in another state.

It was December 25th, and I was still tucked away, cozy in my mother's belly. Little did I know, I was about to be born into a moment of absurd, yet dramatic competition that would define my story long before I took my first breath. The nurses, the doctors, everyone in that hospital room in Atlanta, Georgia, had their eyes on me—and their ears on some kind of mysterious baby radar, because according to them, I wasn't just about to be born, I was about to be the first Christmas baby born in the United States.

Yes, you read that right. Somewhere, in some far-off hospital in some unknown state, another woman was in labor, too. And for reasons I still don't quite understand, the nurses in my mom's delivery room were fully aware of it.

How? Don't ask me. Were they all somehow telepathically linked to birthing rooms across the country? I mean, how exactly does a hospital staff in Georgia know what's happening in delivery rooms in Maine or Texas? They wouldn't tell me, so don't ask. All I know is that my poor mother was caught up in an unintended birthing competition with another woman she'd never met—and the nurses were practically cheering her on as if she was running in the Olympic games.

"Push! We have to win!"

Now, let's pause here for a moment because, honestly, this entire scenario still feels unreal to me. But if you were to ask anyone in my family, they would all nod and confirm that this is exactly how it went down. My arrival wasn't just special because I was born on Christmas Day; it was special because I was about to be part of something bigger—a Christmas Day race that would become a family legend.

Spoiler alert: I didn't quite win that race. Some other baby—no doubt just as special—managed to beat me to the finish line in another state, but I was close. And for my family, that was enough. I became their Christmas miracle, a child they never expected, but one who would change everything.

A Gift No One Saw Coming

The funny part about my birth is that it almost didn't happen—not the Christmas Day part, but the whole thing. You see, I wasn't planned. I was more of a divine plot twist in my parents' lives. I'm the sixth child in a family that, by that point, was very much done with babies. In fact, my mom went to the doctor specifically to make sure there would be no more children. Her plan was to have her tubes tied—no more pregnancies, no more late-night feedings, no more diapers. She had made up her mind, but fate, it seemed, had other plans.

When my mom sat in that doctor's office, waiting to be told she was free of future pregnancies, the doctor hesitated outside the door, nervous. I can only imagine the scene: a doctor, knowing full well what news he's about to deliver, probably preparing himself for a range of emotions from disbelief to anger. When he finally entered, he did so carefully, standing just inside the doorway—ready to flee if necessary.

"Mrs. Walls, I can't tie your tubes today… because, well, you're pregnant."

Pregnant? My mom probably couldn't believe it. I mean, imagine going in to end your baby-making days only to be told that you're already making another one. The irony would have been laughable if it wasn't happening to her. She was shocked, to say the least. This wasn't part of the plan.

She thought about terminating the pregnancy. After all, with five children already—four boys and one girl, mind you—adding another one to the mix seemed overwhelming. But then something happened that would change the course of both our lives forever.

A Dream That Changed Everything

One night, my mom had a dream, but this wasn't just any ordinary dream. In this dream, an angel appeared. The angel, silent and serene, gently laid a baby—me— on a fireplace, then walked away, leaving me there, resting, alive and warm.

When my mom woke up from that dream, she knew she couldn't go through with the abortion. She believed God had spoken to her, showing her that I was meant to be. And once she made that decision, the gears of fate clicked into place. My life, which almost wasn't, became destined to be.

God, it seemed, had other plans, and what better way to cement those plans than by having me born on the most symbolic day of the year—Christmas Day? It was as if God wanted to remind my mother of the gift of life, and I became that gift, wrapped in the perfect package of a December 25th birth.

The Last of the Six Children

So, there I was—the final child, the grand finale. Four boys, one girl, and me, the baby of the family. My older siblings already had stories of their own, each one larger than life, but now it was my turn to enter the family, to make my mark in the ongoing saga of the Walls household. My arrival may have been unplanned, but it was far from unwanted, at least once my mom had made her peace with the idea.

My siblings, though? Well, that's another story.

As the youngest, I had a front-row seat to all the drama that comes with being part of a big family. Five boys and one girl meant a lot of chaos—there were fights, loud conversations, wrestling matches in the living room, and enough trouble to fill several childhoods. But with all that chaos came love, and I grew up knowing that no matter what, my family was there for me.

Maybe it was because I was the last baby. Maybe it was because I was born on Christmas. Whatever the reason, my mom often looked at me like I was something more than just her sixth child. I was her reminder of faith; of the choices we don't always understand but trust in anyway. And so, with my birth on that miraculous Christmas morning, the stage was set. My life, already filled with twists and divine interventions before it had even begun, would become a journey of love, loss, resilience, and the kind of drama you only see in movies.

Little did I know, that was just the beginning.

Chapter 2

The Shattered Innocence of Youth

We tend to think that childhood is a time of innocence, a period filled with wonder, discovery, and trust. But for some, childhood is a battlefield—one where innocence isn't just lost but stolen, taken by the very people meant to protect you.

I was five years old, too young to understand the depth of what was happening to me, yet old enough to feel the confusion and fear that crept in like shadows. You see, for a child, the world is simple—family equals safety. Family equals love. So, when members of your own family are the ones who break that sacred trust, it tears apart everything you know.

It started with subtle touches, little moments that felt strange but were explained away. "This is normal," they said. "This is just how families are close," they would whisper in reassuring tones. I didn't know any better. Why would I? They made it seem like a natural part of growing up, and as a young child, all I wanted was to be loved. I wanted to feel special. And that's exactly how they made me feel—special, but for all the wrong reasons.

The manipulation was masterful, so much so that I didn't even realize it was happening. They didn't hurt me, not at first. Instead, they used affection, soft words, and kindness as weapons, chipping away at my sense of reality. The touches became more frequent, lingering in ways that made me uncomfortable, but I was too young to understand why.

They'd tell me how important it was not to share our "secret," and because I was five years old, I believed them. They'd say, "This is just between us. This is how you know you're loved." And when you're five, love is all you want, so you take it in whatever form it's given—even when it's twisted and wrong.

Molestation is not just an invasion of the body—it's an invasion of the mind, the spirit, and the very foundation of who you are. The most dangerous part is how it manipulates your emotions. They made me believe this was normal. They made me feel like this was love, a love so special that no one else could know about it. And they sealed that illusion with rewards—gifts, toys, and treats. I thought I was being good, being rewarded for keeping the secret, for being "special."

But as with all dark secrets, the truth has a way of showing itself eventually. There was a day when everything changed. I remember it so vividly, like a nightmare etched into my soul. It was one of the family members, someone I had trusted implicitly. They pushed things further than ever before, beyond what I thought was normal. For the first time, there was pain. Sharp, searing pain that shocked me out of the fantasy they had constructed around me.

I screamed. I didn't mean to, but the pain forced it out of me, a scream so primal and raw that it seemed to echo through the room. And in that moment, everything shifted. They stopped, but instead of apologizing, instead of comforting me, they lashed out. "Boys don't cry!" They spat at me. "Only girls scream like that!" And then, the cruelest words of all: "If you tell anyone, they'll think you're weak. You'll be sent away. You'll be punished."

I was five, and I believed them. They had already convinced me that this was how boys learned about life. Now they were telling me that if I spoke out, I'd be branded as something weak, something shameful. They called me names— "faggot," "sissy," "little girl"—words that cut deeper than any of the physical pain. They made me feel like I was less than, like I was something disgusting, something unworthy of love.

That's the insidious nature of abuse. It makes you question everything—your worth, your identity, your

12

very sense of self. It plants seeds of shame and guilt that grow into thorns, wrapping around your heart and squeezing the life out of it. I felt trapped, unable to speak, unable to fight back, because I thought I was the one in the wrong. After all, I had kept the secret. I had let it happen. So, in my young, confused mind, wasn't I just as guilty?

From that moment on, I retreated into myself. I became withdrawn, introverted, unwilling to trust anyone. I started to avoid family gatherings, afraid that it would happen again. I stopped wanting to spend the night with relatives, even the ones who hadn't hurt me, because I didn't know who I could trust anymore. It wasn't long before I became the kid who cried at sleepovers, begging to go home, because home was the only place that felt safe.

My parents didn't know what was wrong. They had no idea what had been happening behind closed doors. To them, I was just becoming a shy, quiet boy. They didn't know the storm that was raging inside

13

me, the whirlwind of fear, confusion, and shame that was pulling me under. And because I didn't have the words to explain it, I kept it all inside.

That's the thing about molestation—it doesn't just hurt you in the moment. It creates a lasting ripple effect, a deep wound that festers and spreads throughout your life. It changes the way you see the world, the way you see yourself. I started to believe that maybe I wasn't worth protecting. Maybe I deserved what happened to me. Maybe I was broken in some fundamental way.

The psychological toll of abuse is something that can follow you for years, sometimes for a lifetime. It disrupts and destabilizes your ability to trust, to form healthy relationships, to even understand what love really means. I carried that weight with me for a long time, too afraid to share it, too afraid to confront it. And as I moved through my childhood, it became a part of me, a secret burden that shaped every decision I made.

I hid behind jokes, using humor as a shield to deflect attention away from the pain. I became the class clown, always ready with a quick joke or a funny comment, because if people were laughing, they weren't looking too closely at the brokenness inside me. It was a mask, a way of coping, but deep down, I was still that scared little boy, hiding from the world.

But the trauma didn't just stop at emotional withdrawal. It seeped into every part of my life, affecting how I saw my body, how I interacted with others, and how I viewed my own masculinity. I was constantly trying to prove I wasn't weak, that I wasn't the "sissy" they had called me. I overcompensated, trying to be tough, trying to live up to some warped idea of what it meant to be a man.

The truth is, molestation leaves you with scars that run deeper than any physical injury. It shakes the foundation of who you are, making you question your value, your worth, and your place in the world.

And for me, it created a battle I didn't know how to fight, a war that raged silently inside me for years.

Even now, as I look back on those years, I can see how much it shaped me. It made me cautious, always on edge, always wondering who I could trust and who I couldn't. It made me question myself, doubt my abilities, and shy away from opportunities because I didn't believe I was worthy of them. It took me years— decades, really—to unravel the damage, to heal from the pain, and to learn how to trust again.

But healing is possible. That's the most important thing I want people to know. No matter how deep the wounds go, no matter how broken you feel, you can heal. It takes time, it takes strength, and it takes courage, but it's possible. I'm living proof of that. I've fought my way through the darkness, through the shame and the guilt, and I've come out on the other side.

There's a long road ahead, and the scars will always be there, but they no longer define me. I am more than what happened to me. I am more than the pain I endured. And as I grew older, the boy with big dreams and even bigger struggles, I began to realize that my story wasn't over. It was just beginning.

Chapter 3

The Boy with Big Dreams and Bigger Struggles

From the outside looking in, I was just a quiet, smart kid with potential that everyone could see. But if you peeled back the layers, you'd discover a different story, one that wasn't as bright as my report cards or as perfect as my teachers thought.

Inside, I was a boy battling more than just school assignments—I was wrestling with a version of myself that I thought the world saw and hated.

It started early, probably around kindergarten, when kids first began to notice differences—anything that didn't fit their idea of "normal." For me, it was my hands. I had big hands. Even then, they didn't quite match the rest of my body, and to the other kids, they became the perfect target. The teasing started out small. It was just a few kids, here and there, who'd snicker and point.

"Hey, big hands!"

"You going to play basketball with those hands?"

I laughed it off at first. It was innocent enough, right? But kids have a way of latching onto something and running with it until it turns into something much bigger than it ever should have been. By the time I hit first grade, it wasn't just my hands anymore. My nose had grown, too—at least in their eyes—and suddenly, I had two new nicknames: Big Hands and Big Nose.

It didn't help that I was already a naturally introverted kid. Socializing wasn't easy for me, so when the bullying began, I didn't know how to defend myself. My first instinct was to shrink into myself, to make myself invisible so that no one could see what was obvious to them—these flaws they'd found in me. But it didn't work. Kids have a radar for weakness, and I was a beacon.

The Weight of Being Different

Every day at school was like stepping into a battlefield, except I wasn't armed with anything. I wasn't the tough kid who fought back or the cool kid who could brush it off. I was the kid who wore my heart on my sleeve, who took every comment and jab like it was a personal failure.

"You could smell us all from here with that nose!"

"Why don't you reach for that with your giant hands?"

The jokes were constant, and no matter how much I tried to ignore them, they seeped into my bones, into my mind, until I couldn't see myself the way my parents or my teachers did. All I saw was a kid who didn't belong, a boy with oversized hands and a nose that felt like it took up half my face.

In truth, my hands weren't even that big. My nose? Sure, it had some character to it, but it was nothing like they made it out to be. But when you're a kid, perception becomes your reality. And my reality was that I was weird, abnormal, and destined to be the butt of every joke.

The Clown Behind the Pain

By second grade, I had developed a survival strategy. If they were going to laugh at me, then I'd give them something to laugh at—on my terms. It was around this time that I discovered my talent for humor, or rather, I discovered that if I made people laugh, they didn't seem to care as much about my nose or my hands.

So, I became the class clown. I was the one who cracked jokes when the teacher's back was turned, who made funny faces during lessons, who tripped over my own feet on purpose just to hear the room explode with laughter. But it wasn't the laughter that made me feel better—it was the control. For the first time, I wasn't just the kid with the big hands and big nose—I was funny. I was the kid who made people laugh. It was a trade-off, and to me, it felt like a better deal. If I couldn't be normal, then at least I could be the clown.

What no one realized, though, was that behind every joke, behind every silly face and exaggerated pratfall, there was a boy who was hiding. Hiding from the taunts, hiding from the judgment, and more than anything, hiding from himself.

A Hidden Genius

At home, things were different. My parents, bless them, never understood why I struggled so much at school. They saw the grades—the straight A's, the glowing comments from teachers about my intelligence and my creativity—and they were proud. They didn't see the boy who walked through the hallways of his school with his head down, hoping no one would notice him.

I was, as they liked to say, "destined for greatness." They weren't wrong—I was smart. Schoolwork came easy to me. I could solve math problems in my head before the teacher had finished writing them on the board. I had a creative streak that was impossible to contain, filled with ideas, inventions, and stories that played out like movies in my mind. But none of that seemed to matter when I was sitting in the cafeteria, surrounded by kids who thought I was nothing more than a walking joke.

I spent most of my early years hiding my talents from the world. I didn't want to stand out for the wrong reasons, so I buried the parts of myself that could have made me shine. Instead, I leaned into the humor, into the persona I had created— the clown. If they were going to look at me, I'd at least control why they were looking.

I laughed on the outside, but on the inside, I carried the weight of every joke, every nickname, every sneer. It was like walking around with an invisible backpack full of rocks, each one a reminder that I was different, that I didn't quite fit in. But I carried it because, back then, it felt like I didn't have a choice.

The Isolation of Genius

For an introverted kid, being in a large family was both a blessing and a curse. At home, I could disappear among my siblings. I didn't have to be front and center, and there was comfort in that. But there was also loneliness. With five older siblings—most of them boisterous and loud—I often felt like I was fading into the background. My thoughts, my ideas, the things that made me me—they were all tucked away, buried beneath the noise of a big household and the constant buzz of life happening around me.

I found solace in my own world, in my thoughts. I'd lose myself in books, in drawing, in building things out of scraps I found lying around the house. I created worlds in my head where I wasn't the kid with the big nose and big hands, where I was the hero, the inventor, the creator of things that people marveled at. But those worlds stayed in my head, locked away because I didn't have the courage to share them. At school, I was a clown. At home, I was the quiet one. And in both places, I felt alone.

A Storm Brewing

Looking back, it's clear that those early years shaped me in ways I didn't understand at the time. The seeds of insecurity had been planted, and though I didn't know it then, they would take root and grow, wrapping themselves around my identity like vines. I was a kid who had been told he was special—by his parents, by his teachers, by everyone who saw his potential—but I didn't believe it. I couldn't.

I had spent too much time being told that my worth was tied to things I couldn't control—my appearance, my quirks, my differences. And so, I kept hiding, kept diverting attention with humor, kept shrinking into myself.

But there was a storm brewing. It wasn't the kind of storm you can see on the horizon, with dark clouds and rumbling thunder. It was the kind of storm that starts deep inside, slowly gathering strength, waiting for the right moment to break.

And when it did, everything would change.

Chapter 4

Love, Anger, and the Lessons of a Shattered Moment

Home is supposed to be a sanctuary, a place where love thrives and grows. For most of us, that's the dream—the ideal. But my home was a paradox. It was a place filled with music and laughter, the hum of joy that threaded through our days. Yet, it was also a place where, at times, anger and violence crept in like an unwelcome guest, tearing at the edges of that happiness, leaving behind scars that I didn't fully understand until I was older.

It was around the second grade when I began to notice the duality in my parents' relationship. They loved each other—there was no doubt about that. I could see it in their laughter, in the way they danced around the kitchen to old R&B songs, and in the way they held hands during Sunday dinners. My father's deep baritone voice would fill the house, singing along to Al Green or The Temptations, while my mother's infectious laughter would echo, making all of us kids feel like we were part of something bigger, something special.

But love is a complicated thing. It doesn't always look the way it should. For every moment of joy, there seemed to be a moment of tension—a side of my parents that made love seem like a dangerous game. They would fight. Not just small arguments but full-blown battles, words slung like weapons, tearing at the seams of whatever peace we had. It was a strange kind of love, one that could go from warm and tender to cold and sharp in the blink of an eye. It confused me, as it would any child, and left me wondering what love was really supposed to look like.

One moment stands out, a moment that would shape me, alter my perception of love, and leave an imprint on my heart that I would carry for years to come.

I was in the second grade. My days were filled with schoolwork, recess, and dreams about the future. But home was unpredictable, and you never quite knew what you were walking into when you came through the door. That night, it was one of those nights where the tension in the air was so thick, it felt like you could cut it with a knife.

I was sitting at the kitchen table, doing my homework, when I heard them start to argue in the next room. It was nothing new—fights between them had become part of the rhythm of our home. At first, I didn't pay much attention, too focused on my math problems to notice the shift in their voices. But then I heard my father's voice rise above the rest.

"You ain't nothing but a b***h," he spat out, his voice filled with venom.

And then I heard my mother's voice, calm yet laced with a warning I hadn't heard before: "If you call me that again, I swear to God, I'm going to shoot you."

For a split second, everything went silent, like the air had been sucked out of the room. And then it happened—the bang that would change everything.

My father had started to say the word again, the one that was like gasoline to my mother's fire. But he never finished it. Instead, there was a deafening sound, a bang that echoed through the house, loud enough to make the walls tremble. It was the sound of my mother's gun, fired at close range, straight into my father's chest.

Everything moved in slow motion after that. My father staggered backward, clutching his chest as blood soaked through his shirt. My mother stood there, frozen, the gun still in her hand. Her face was a mask of disbelief, her body trembling with shock. The weight of what she had done, what anger had driven her to do, crashed over her like a wave. She dropped the gun and ran into the bathroom, slamming the door behind her. I could hear her sobs through the walls, raw and full of regret.

32

It wasn't supposed to happen like this. My mother wasn't supposed to shoot the man she loved. But in that moment, fueled by anger and hurt, she had done the unthinkable. And she couldn't take it back.

My older brother, quick to act, rushed to my father's side. He didn't hesitate—he picked him up, blood still pouring from the wound, and dragged him out to the car. I stood there, too stunned to move, too young to understand what was really happening. All I knew was that something had shifted in my world, something had broken.

At the hospital, my father—still protecting the woman who had just shot him—told the doctors that he had been cleaning his gun and it had accidentally gone off. He didn't blame her. He didn't press charges. In his own twisted way, that was his love for her—a love that could withstand even a bullet. But what kind of love was that? I wondered. What kind of love could survive violence like this?

I admired their love, but I feared it too. I didn't want to duplicate it, to become the kind of person who thought that love and pain had to walk hand in hand. But witnessing it did something to me. It normalized the idea that the people who love you are supposed to hurt you. That somehow, love wasn't real if it didn't come with some kind of suffering.

For a long time after that, I struggled with the concept of love. I thought that maybe all love was like this— a mix of beauty and violence, laughter and tears, joy, and heartbreak. I thought that maybe to be truly loved, you had to endure the pain that came with it. It was a belief that would take years to unlearn, but at that moment, as a second grader standing in the aftermath of my parents' fight, it felt like the truth.

The strangest part was that even though I saw them fight, even though I heard the words they hurled at each other and saw the violence that sometimes erupted between them, I knew they loved each other. There was no denying that. It was a complicated,

34

messy love, but it was real. And they loved us—my siblings and me—with the same fierceness, the same passion. They would die for us, I knew that. But sometimes, that love came with pain.

Witnessing that moment did something to me. It fractured something deep inside, making me question what love really was. But despite everything, despite the normalization of hurt, I couldn't bring myself to harm others. My heart was different. I didn't want to perpetuate the cycle of pain I had grown up seeing. I couldn't. I wanted something more, something better. But that didn't stop the confusion, didn't stop the deep-rooted belief that somehow, love and hurt were two sides of the same coin.

As I grew older, I would carry that with me—this idea that love was complicated, messy, and sometimes painful. But I would also learn that it didn't have to be. Love could be kind, it could be gentle, it could be patient. And that's what I would strive for, even as the echoes of that bang, the sound of a love that almost ended in tragedy, would stay with me for years to come.

Chapter 5

The Choir of Pain and Praise

As I moved into late elementary school and eventually middle school, the constant bullying that had defined much of my early years finally began to ease. The taunts and laughter about my nose, my hands, and my body were no longer the relentless soundtrack of my life. The jokes about my appearance slowly faded, and, in their place, a new identity emerged. The class clown. The one who could make everyone laugh, not because they found me weird, but because I wanted them to. It was a way to control the narrative, a defense mechanism that allowed me to hide my pain in plain sight.

I became more popular in school—not in the traditional sense of popularity, but in the way that I was the guy who could lighten the mood with a joke or make the class burst into laughter when things got too serious. It was easier to be known for my humor than for the trauma that lurked beneath. But no matter how much I joked or how many people I made laugh, the truth was always there. I was still the same boy who had been hurt, who was hiding behind his laughter because it was safer than confronting the pain.

As I grew older, I began to explore relationships, dating and having girlfriends like other boys my age. On the surface, everything looked normal—I had friends, I had crushes, I was doing all the things teenagers were supposed to do. But behind it all was the trauma I had carried with me since I was young. The memories of being molested by family members cast a shadow over every relationship. I couldn't escape the feeling that something was wrong with me, that I wasn't like the other boys, that love and intimacy came with a cost that I didn't fully understand.

Despite these feelings, I found an outlet, a place where I could escape from the heaviness of the world, even if only for a little while: the church. The

38

sanctuary, where I could turn to God, became a lifeline. I joined the church choir, a decision that would change the course of my life. In the choir, I discovered something I didn't know I had—a gift for singing, a voice that seemed to be waiting to be uncovered. I didn't just sing because it was expected in church; I sang because it gave me peace, a way to connect with God in a deeply personal and spiritual way.

Music became my refuge. Through singing, I found a way to express emotions I couldn't put into words. The hurt, the confusion, the anger—it all found a place in the melodies I sang and the lyrics I began to write. I discovered I had a talent for writing songs, for crafting words that echoed the feelings I held deep inside. It was like opening a door to a part of me that had been locked away. Music became my therapy, my form of worship, and, most importantly, my connection to a God who I believed was still watching over me, even through all the pain.

But even in the place where I should've found the most safety, I faced a different kind of danger. The youth choir director, a man I should have trusted as a mentor, began to make advances. They were subtle at first, compliments that went beyond the typical praise of a choir leader, lingering touches that felt more invasive than supportive. I knew this feeling too well from my childhood, and it triggered something in me, a warning bell that kept going off.

I became hyper-aware of my surroundings at church, always making sure that I was never alone with him. I loved being in the choir, I loved singing and connecting to God, but now, church wasn't just about worship—it became a place where I had to guard myself. There was a constant tension between wanting to be there, to experience the joy and peace that music brought me, and wanting to avoid the advances that lurked in the background.

It was a kind of mental torment. On the one hand, I had found this beautiful gift of singing and writing, a

40

way to escape the pain of the world, to lose myself in melodies and praise. On the other hand, the very place that should've been my sanctuary also harbored someone I needed to protect myself from. It was exhausting. Every Sunday, I felt like I was preparing for battle—not just spiritual warfare, but a literal fight for my personal safety.

I never told anyone about what was happening—not my parents, not my friends. Part of me was ashamed, afraid that I would be seen as weak for letting it affect me. The other part felt it was easier to manage it on my own, to control the situation by keeping it to myself. But it didn't make it any less painful.

And yet, through it all, I never left the church. There was something about the connection I felt to God when I sang that was stronger than any fear or discomfort I experienced. Despite the advances, despite the mental strain, I knew that my faith was real. I held onto it, even when it seemed like everything around me was falling apart.

Being in the choir introduced me to a deeper form of worship. It was there that I learned that worship wasn't just about singing songs or going through the motions. It was about connecting to something bigger than myself. In those moments of praise, I felt like God was speaking to me, reminding me that I wasn't alone in my struggles. Those moments gave me the strength to endure the hurt, the trauma, and the advances I faced, both in the church and in life.

But no matter how much joy I found in my music and faith, I couldn't shake the weight of my past. The trauma I carried from childhood was still there, lingering in the background of every decision I made. I dated, I had girlfriends, but intimacy still frightened me. How could I open up to anyone when I hadn't fully processed the pain I'd been carrying for so long?

It was a delicate balancing act—pretending everything was fine, keeping up appearances, making people laugh, all while dealing with the emotional and mental burden of my past. And yet, I kept going. I sang. I worshiped. I found strength in my faith.

The more I sang, the more I realized that my connection to God was stronger than anything else in my life. And while church wasn't always the safe haven I hoped it would be, it became the place where I found myself. It was where I discovered my voice—both literally and figuratively—and where I began to understand that no matter what I had been through, there was a plan for my life. Even through the pain, I still found hope.

As I transitioned from late middle into high school, the challenges of my past were still there, but I was beginning to see a new path forward. One filled with music, faith, and the possibility of healing.

Even though the bullying had lessened, and I was starting to make friends, the trauma of my past still clung to me. But I was learning how to navigate it—

one song, one prayer, one step at a time. And while it would take many more years to fully confront the pain I carried, this chapter of my life showed me that even in the darkest places, God could still shine a light.

It was a light I would need to hold onto tightly as I entered a new phase of my life—a phase where the battles would be different, but the stakes would be just as high.

Chapter 6

Falling into Darkness, Reaching for Light

High school was a mix of highs and lows for me, both literally and figuratively. It started off like a dream, a period where things were finally coming together. After the bullying I had endured throughout elementary and middle school, I had finally found my footing. I joined the marching band, and that gave me a sense of identity and belonging that I had longed for. I was no longer the kid hiding behind jokes and nervous laughter. I was cool now—one of the popular kids. No more teasing, no more feeling like an outsider. It felt good to be accepted for once.

I even started dating here and there, having a few girlfriends, but no matter how hard I tried, the trauma from my childhood lingered. It was like a shadow that followed me everywhere, never letting me forget the experiences I had endured. On the outside, I had become the kid everyone wanted to hang out with, but on the inside, I was still struggling with my self-worth and the scars that no one could see. Relationships were tough because intimacy terrified me. I would often push people away before they could get too close, afraid that they would see the brokenness I had worked so hard to hide.

Despite these challenges, my early high school years were filled with promise. I was doing well academically and had a bright future ahead of me. But that all changed as I transitioned into my junior year. Things began to shift. I started smoking marijuana—at first, just casually, just a way to unwind and relax. But before long, it became a regular thing. I was getting high more often, skipping school, and eventually, it all caught up to me. I lost focus on my academics, and I lost the momentum I had built in the first couple of years. Eventually, I got expelled.

It was the beginning of a downward spiral. With school no longer a priority, I started looking for other ways to occupy my time. The streets offered quick money, and I started selling drugs—not because I wanted to live a criminal lifestyle, but because I saw it as a fast way to make money without the responsibility of having to hold down a job or go to school. I wasn't in a gang, but I was close enough to it that it could have gone either way. My faith in God, though weakened, was still there, pulling me back from the edge. It was like an invisible force that kept me from going all the way into the darkness.

Around this time, I also started drinking alcohol— heavily. I would drink with family, with friends, and no one really knew what I was getting into. To my parents, I was still their good kid, the one who was finding his way after a tough start. But the truth was, I was hiding a lot from them. I didn't want them to see the mess I was making of my life.

As the drugs and alcohol became more of a crutch, I started experimenting with other substances— ecstasy, pills, anything that could give me an escape from the pain I was trying so hard to avoid. One night, everything came to a head. I was out with friends, partying, drinking, and using drugs like it was nothing. But this night was different. I was drugged without fully realizing what was happening, and I found myself in a situation that shattered the very foundations of what I believed to be normal. I was high out of my mind, and I participated in something that went against everything I thought I stood for.

It was a sexual act that crossed boundaries I didn't even know I had. When I woke up the next morning, the weight of what had happened was heavy. I couldn't remember everything, but the pieces I could recall were enough to make me feel ashamed, guilty, and completely lost. I had let my guard down, and in doing so, I had opened the door to a lifestyle that was never meant for me. A lifestyle where both genders of the human species, both male and female became a lustful appetite that was both enjoyed and hated. I felt as though I had crossed into a world that didn't align with my faith or upbringing, and yet I was now entangled in it.

This night opened a door that led to even darker places. I started partying more, getting high just to escape the reality of what my life had become. I would get so high that I wouldn't remember anything the next day, and in some twisted way, that made it easier for me to live with myself. I could tell myself that I didn't really know what had happened because I couldn't remember it, so maybe it wasn't as bad as it seemed. But the truth was, I knew deep down that I was spiraling, and it was only a matter of time before something went terribly wrong.

Girlfriends came and went during this time, and I found myself engaging in relationships that were more about escaping reality than building any real connection. I remember one girlfriend who introduced me to swinging parties, places where anything went. She would drug me beforehand—at my request—so that I wouldn't remember the things we did. It was easier that way. I wouldn't have to face the reality of the situation the next morning. But with every night like this, I lost more and more of myself. It felt like I was giving pieces of my soul away, piece by piece, until there was nothing left.

The deeper I got into this lifestyle, the more I hated myself. I wanted to stop, but I didn't know how. I was so far in that I didn't see a way out. I was living a double life—still connected to the church, still holding onto my faith, but also deeply entrenched in a world of drugs, sex, and fast money. I was trying to please God, but I was also feeding my flesh, and the two worlds were at war within me.

One night, everything came to a head. I had gotten so high that I felt like I was on the verge of dying. My heart raced, my mind spun, and I could feel myself slipping away. In that moment, I had to make a decision. Did I want to live, or did I want to die? And in the quietest part of my soul, I knew I wanted to live. I didn't know how to climb out of the hole I had dug for myself, but I knew I deserved to live, even after everything I had done.

After that night, I started to pull back from the drugs and the partying, but the scars remained. I was still dealing with the trauma of my past, and even though I wasn't as heavily involved in the things I had once been, the damage had already been done. I wasn't using drugs as much, but I found myself addicted to other things— things that would haunt me for years to come.

But even through all of this, God had a plan for me. I didn't see it then, but I would come to realize that the path I had walked, no matter how dark, was part of a greater story. A story of redemption, of finding light in the darkest of places, and of reclaiming the life that was always meant for me.

Chapter 7
The Pillar with Cracks

After years of chaos, heartache, and rebellion, I found myself standing on a new foundation, one that felt stable beneath my feet for the first time in years. It wasn't perfect—there were still lingering pieces of the old me that hadn't fully fallen away—but I had begun to rebuild. I had secured a stable job, and for the first time in a long while, I felt like I had a clear sense of purpose. My connection to God, which had always been present, became deeper and more meaningful. I began to immerse myself in the church, not just as an attendee but as a true participant in ministry.

I was still battling demons—addictions, temptations, and the trauma that continued to hover in the background—but I was no longer drowning in them. I was learning how to swim, how to keep my head above water, and how to push forward. Smoking and drinking were still a part of my life, but it was nothing like the reckless behavior I had indulged in during my younger years. I was growing, evolving, and finding a balance between the person I had been and the person I wanted to be.

As my spiritual life deepened, I found myself more and more committed to my church community. I began feeding the homeless, volunteering at events, and finding any way I could to give back to those in need. Helping others became my new high, a feeling of fulfillment that replaced the emptiness I had once filled with drugs, alcohol, and reckless behavior. There was something transformative about standing in front of a line of people in need, handing out food, offering a smile, and knowing that even in the smallest way, I was making a difference. It wasn't about recognition or praise—it was about serving, about walking in the footsteps of the faith I was trying so hard to embrace.

My relationship with God became more personal than ever before. I wasn't just going through the motions of religion—I was building a spiritual relationship that meant something to me. I started reading the Bible regularly, not just as a book of rules but as a source of guidance, comfort, and wisdom. I would spend nights reflecting on the stories within its pages, finding connections to my own life, my own struggles. The words of scripture began to shape me in ways I hadn't expected. It wasn't just about knowing the verses—it was about living them.

My faith took on a new significance in my life. It became the lens through which I viewed the world, the filter that colored my actions and decisions. Faith wasn't just a set of beliefs—it was my foundation. It was the thing that held me up when the weight of my past threatened to drag me down. I began to understand that God wasn't some distant figure watching from above, waiting to judge me for my mistakes. He was with me, beside me, walking through the valleys of my life, offering grace, forgiveness, and love. It was this understanding that started to change me.

As I grew deeper in my relationship with God, I found myself sinning less. Not because I was striving for perfection, but because my heart was changing. The more I connected with God, the less I wanted to engage in the behaviors that had once consumed me. The desires to drink, smoke, and engage in reckless behavior started to fade. I no longer needed those vices to feel whole. I was finding peace in a higher purpose, in a relationship with a God who loved me despite all my flaws.

This journey with God also led me to become more compassionate and understanding of others. I realized that everyone was on their own path, their own journey, and whether they were in a good place or a bad place, they were still deserving of love and acceptance. I became an advocate for being a better person, not just for myself but for others as well. I started to forgive more easily, to walk in grace, and to set healthy boundaries without shutting people out. I learned that loving someone didn't mean tolerating their bad behavior—it meant holding them accountable while still offering forgiveness and understanding.

One of the biggest steps in my journey was learning to forgive the family members who had created so much of the childhood trauma I had endured. For years, I had carried the weight of anger, shame, and confusion, unsure of how to process the things that had been done to me. But as I walked deeper in my faith, I began to see that holding onto that anger was only hurting me. Forgiveness wasn't about letting them off the hook—it was about freeing myself from the chains of my past. So, I made the choice to forgive. Not because they deserved it, but because I deserved peace.

Through all of this, I became the person my family and friends could depend on. I was the one people came to for prayer, for advice, for support. It was an honor to be that person, to be seen as someone strong, reliable, and spiritually grounded. But it also came with a cost. Being needed became my new high, and just like any high, it left me drained. I loved being there for others, but when I needed help, I often found myself standing alone. Whether it was finances, time, or just a listening ear, there was rarely anyone there for me.

People thought I was naïve or too generous, that I didn't know I was being used. But I knew. I knew exactly what was happening, and I allowed it. In some ways, I felt like it was my purpose. But in time, the weight of always being the one to give and never receiving anything in return began to wear me down. I had become an instrument everyone used without permission, and though I loved helping others, I realized I was neglecting myself in the process.

But God had been working on me, slowly guiding me to a place of self-awareness. I began to set boundaries, to pull back from the things that were draining me. I started focusing on myself again, on my own healing and growth. I began writing more, recording music, and rediscovering the things that brought me joy. I learned to mask the pain, to push it to a corner of my mind where it couldn't control me. I had mastered the art of survival.

But just like any high, the feeling of being needed eventually led to a crash. I realized that I had to stop allowing others to drain me. So, I made a choice. I began to separate myself from the things that were familiar—family, friends, obligations. I still helped people, but only at my own discretion. I needed to reclaim my life, to put myself first for once.

I was in a relationship at the time, but even that felt like something I was outgrowing. Secretly, I began preparing for an escape. I was planning to end the relationship and move out of town to start fresh, to rebuild my life in a place where I could focus solely on my own healing and growth.

And then came the call. The call to fatherhood. Little did I know, everything I had been through, all the trials and tribulations, were preparing me for this moment. A moment that would change my life in ways I could have never imagined. The moment when I would step into a role I had never anticipated but would soon become the defining chapter of my life.

Chapter 8

The Call to Fatherhood

When my phone rang that day, I had no idea it would change my life forever. It was a typical afternoon. The sky outside was overcast, and the air felt heavy—as if it was holding its breath, waiting for something to happen. I had settled into the routine of my life, a routine that, while comfortable, was far from fulfilling. I was in a relationship that lacked real passion, just going through the motions. My job, though stable, gave me no sense of purpose. It paid the bills but left me feeling hollow at the end of each day. I had dreams—big dreams—but they felt like distant stars, twinkling just out of reach.

Then my phone buzzed, breaking the stillness. It was my brother. His voice on the other end was frail, hollowed out by sickness and years of strain. But beyond the rasp of his voice, there was something deeper—an urgency, a plea that gripped me before he even got the words out.

He wasn't calling for himself, even though I knew his health was in a rapid decline. He was calling for his grandsons—my great-nephews. The boys had been through so much already, and now they were in desperate need of help. My brother explained how their father had lost control—again—and lashed out in a fit of rage. This wasn't the first time, and it was unlikely to be the last. My niece, their mother, had her own struggles—her life was unraveling, and she couldn't protect them anymore.

"They need you," he whispered, his voice almost cracking. "Can you take them? Just for a while... until we figure something out."

His words hung in the air like a storm cloud, heavy and full of dread. My heart pounded in my chest as the weight of what he was asking sank in. Could I do this? I wasn't a father. I didn't know the first thing about raising children, let alone boys who had been shattered by trauma and abuse. Fear gnawed at the edges of my resolve, but then I thought of their faces—the faces of my great-nephews, who had already seen too much darkness for children their age.

"I'll take them," I said, without a second thought, even though uncertainty and fear were already clawing at me. How could I say no? They were family. And if there was one thing I knew, it was that family looks out for family, no matter the cost.

When they arrived on my doorstep later that evening, my heart ached. The boys, small and fragile, stood there clutching each other. Their eyes were wide, haunted by fear, searching for some sign that they were finally safe. I knelt down to their level, hoping to ease their nerves with a smile, but it felt strained. Inside, I was as lost as they were. "You're safe now," I said softly, hoping that by saying it, I could somehow make it true.

That first night, after they had fallen asleep—curled up together like two scared kittens—I sat on the couch in the darkness, my mind racing. What had I just agreed to? How was I going to provide the safety and security they needed when I barely knew what I was doing? I wasn't a father, not by any stretch of the imagination. The weight of it all pressed down on me, suffocating me with doubt. But as I sat there in the quiet, I made a silent promise: I would not fail them. No matter how unprepared I was, no matter how difficult the road ahead might be, I would figure it out. I had to. They were counting on me.

What started as a temporary arrangement soon became something much more permanent. The days turned into weeks, the weeks into months, and before I knew it, I had become their father in every way that mattered. But the journey was far from easy. The boys carried deep scars, not just physically, but emotionally. They had been broken by the very people who were supposed to protect them. And though I did everything in my power to show them love and care, the wounds they carried weren't ones that could be easily healed.

There were sleepless nights where I questioned everything. How was I supposed to guide them through their pain when I was still grappling with my own? How could I teach them to trust again when the world had shown them so much betrayal? But I knew I couldn't let my doubts consume me. I had to be strong for them. And in doing so, I found a strength within myself that I never knew existed.

It wasn't long before tensions started to rise within the family. My niece's side— her mother's family— wasn't thrilled that I had taken the boys in. They felt slighted, believing that they should have been given the opportunity to raise them. But my niece, despite her own struggles, had always been closer to our side of the family, and she trusted us to do what was best for her sons. Still, the whispers and side comments came. I felt the sting of their resentment at family gatherings, the quiet disapproval in their eyes as if I had somehow stolen the boys from them.

It was a difficult time, navigating the family politics, trying to reassure everyone that I was doing what was best for the boys, even though my heart was heavy with the weight of it all. There were moments when I questioned whether I had made the right choice, but every time I looked into the boys' eyes and saw the flicker of trust growing, I knew I couldn't turn back.

The road ahead was filled with challenges I never could have imagined, but it was also filled with moments of profound connection, of joy that I hadn't expected. I was learning what it truly meant to be a father—not just in name, but in action. The late-night talks, the comforting of nightmares, the small victories when they smiled or laughed freely for the first time—those were the moments that showed me I was on the right path.

The call to fatherhood had been one of the most terrifying moments of my life. But it was also the beginning of something far greater than I could have ever anticipated. Little did I know, this journey was just getting started. The boys had been through so much, but so had I. Together, we were navigating this new world, trying to heal, trying to find peace. And though the road was long, I knew one thing for sure—I wouldn't trade it for anything.

This was only the beginning.

Chapter 9

The Weight of Single Fatherhood

Becoming a single father overnight wasn't just a shift in my life—it was a transformation that came without warning. It was like waking up one day and finding yourself in the middle of a storm, with no compass, no map, and no shelter. One moment, life was somewhat predictable. I had my routines, my small struggles, and my personal battles, but nothing could have prepared me for the whirlwind that was about to sweep through my world. The call came, and with it, the realization that I was now responsible for two young boys who had been through more pain than I could ever imagine.

It's funny how life can change in an instant. One minute, I was comfortable in my own small existence, not really striving for more, just... living. But the moment my brother asked me to take in his grandsons, my great-nephews, everything shifted. Fear crept in—fear of failing them, of not being enough. I knew nothing about being a father. But what I knew was this: they needed me, and I couldn't turn them away.

I quickly learned that being a single father was a balancing act, a constant struggle to keep my head above water. There were nights when the exhaustion hit me like a wave, crashing over me in relentless surges. Physically, I was drained. Sleep became a luxury I couldn't afford. The boys were still so young, so vulnerable, and they had been through enough nightmares already. I couldn't bear the thought of them waking up in the middle of the night, scared, and me not being there. So, I became hyper-aware, listening for the slightest sound, ready to jump out of bed to comfort them at a moment's notice.

But the physical toll was nothing compared to the emotional strain. As the days turned into weeks, the financial pressure mounted. Before the boys came into my life, I had enough to scrape by. My needs

70

were simple, and I didn't worry too much about budgeting. But now, with two growing boys to care for, every penny mattered. I remember the panic that washed over me when I realized just how much everything would cost. School supplies, new clothes, doctor visits—it all added up faster than I could handle. The bills piled up, and no matter how carefully I budgeted, it was never enough.

Then, as if the universe wanted to test me further, my car broke down. I still remember the sinking feeling in my stomach as the engine sputtered and died while I was driving the boys to school. We were stranded on the side of the road, and I felt completely helpless. How was I supposed to get them to school? How was I going to get to work? I didn't have the money to fix the car, let alone buy a new one. I sat there, gripping the steering wheel, my heart pounding in my chest, trying to hold back the tears. Everything felt like it was falling apart.

In moments like that, it was easy to feel like I was failing. The weight of it all—the financial strain, the emotional exhaustion, the fear of letting the boys down—it crushed me. There were nights I would sit at the kitchen table, staring at the bills, wondering how on earth I was going to make it all work. It felt like I was constantly putting out fires, trying to stay one step ahead of the chaos, but I was always just one wrong move away from everything unraveling.

Just when I thought I couldn't take any more, a friend stepped in. She saw the burden I was carrying and offered me her car. "Take it," she said, "use it as long as you need to. Don't worry about the repairs or insurance—just keep gas in it." Her generosity was a lifeline, and it gave me the strength to keep going. For months, I drove that car, grateful for every single mile, knowing that without it, everything would have crumbled. Her act of kindness reminded me that, even in the darkest moments, there are people who will step up and help carry the load.

Still, the financial pressure didn't let up. I became a master at juggling—rationing food, lights, gas, and water, making sure every resource was stretched to its limit. There were days when I had to make the impossible choice between paying a bill or feeding the boys. More often than not, I would skip meals, quietly pushing my plate aside so they could have enough to eat. They were too young to notice or question why I wasn't eating, and I was thankful for that. The truth was, there just wasn't enough to go around.

The emotional toll weighed heavily on me. I couldn't let the boys see how scared I was, how close I was to breaking. They needed me to be strong, to be their rock, but inside, I was unraveling. I would collapse into bed at the end of the day, my body aching, my mind racing, wondering how much longer I could keep this up. But no matter how hard it got; I knew one thing for sure—I couldn't give up. These boys had already lost so much, and I refused to let them lose anything more.

The boys weren't blind to the struggles we faced, though I tried to shield them as much as I could. But despite everything, they flourished in our little makeshift family. They laughed, they played, and they began to trust me. Slowly but surely, we built something together—a home. A home filled with love; despite the challenges we faced. Every time they smiled, every time they wrapped their small arms around me, I knew I was doing something right.

Still, the weight of single fatherhood was relentless. The emotional highs and lows were dizzying. One minute, I felt like I was doing okay—like maybe I was actually succeeding at this impossible task. And the next, I was drowning again, consumed by the fear that I wasn't enough. But through it all, I kept going. I kept showing up, day after day, because I had made a promise. A promise that I would never give up on these boys, no matter how hard it got.

And so, with every struggle, every sleepless night, and every ounce of exhaustion, I carried on. For them.

Chapter 10

The Battle with DFCS

If there's one thing I learned quickly, it's that dealing with DFCS is like being put on trial every single day, for a crime you don't even know you've been accused of. From the moment those boys came into my care, my life was no longer my own. It didn't matter that I had opened my home and heart to them without hesitation. It didn't matter that I had chosen to step up when no one else could. To DFCS, I wasn't a father trying to give his nephews a better life—I was just another case number, another potential failure in their eyes.

Every week, like clockwork, a social worker would knock on my door with that clipboard in hand, her eyes darting around the house as though she were a detective searching for evidence. It didn't matter how many times I'd welcomed them into my home, how many hoops I jumped through—my love, my commitment to those boys was always in question. And every week, I had to prove myself all over again.

The inspections weren't just thorough; they were invasive. They didn't just look— they searched. They opened every cabinet, rifled through drawers, examined closets, and scrutinized every detail of our lives. My home—what should have been our sanctuary—felt like it was under siege. They took pictures of our fridge, counted the food in the pantry, inspected the boys' clothes for wear and tear, and even snapped photos of the bathroom, as though the state of our shower tiles could somehow dictate my ability to be a father.

I felt violated. Exposed. Like my entire existence was under a microscope, and no matter how hard I tried, no matter how many precautions I took, there was always something more to inspect, some new reason for them to doubt me. It didn't matter that the boys were starting to smile again, starting to feel safe after everything they had been through. To the system, they were statistics, and I was just the temporary guardian.

But the worst part—the part that made my stomach twist with anger—was the body checks.

Every single week, like clockwork, my great-nephews were forced to strip down in front of a stranger. A stranger with cold hands and an even colder gaze, who looked them over for any sign of abuse, any new bruise or mark that could be used as evidence against me. Their small, vulnerable bodies—bodies that had already been touched and hurt by the people who were supposed to love them—were put on display. I saw the way their little shoulders would hunch, the way their eyes would dart to the ground, full of shame. It didn't matter how much I tried to comfort them afterward, telling them it was just procedure. The damage was done.

What kind of message was that sending to them? How could I teach them about trust and safety, about ownership of their own bodies, when every week they were reminded that their bodies weren't truly theirs? That at any moment, a stranger could demand to see them, to inspect them, to judge them. And I— powerless to stop it—had to stand by, watching their innocence be chipped away, little by little.

It tore me apart. It broke something inside me that I wasn't sure could ever be mended. I knew, logically, that DFCS was trying to protect them. I knew they were trying to ensure the boys were safe. But the reality of their system was that it often did more harm than good. These boys, who had already been through so much, were being retraumatized, week after week.

And as much as I wanted to scream, to tell them to stop, I knew I couldn't. I had to keep my anger in check. I had to smile and nod, and go through the motions, because if I didn't, if I pushed back, if I refused, they could take the boys away. I couldn't risk that. So, I did what I had to do. I played their game. I filled out their forms, attended their meetings, and submitted to every humiliating inspection. Not because I wanted to, but because I had no other choice. The boys were worth it. They had to be worth it.

But no matter how many hoops I jumped through, it always felt like there was one more. Every meeting brought a new demand, a new requirement, a new way to prove that I was worthy of being a father to these boys. And the worst part? I wasn't even trying to adopt strangers. These boys were my family—my blood. But to DFCS, that didn't matter. The fact that they were my great-nephews seemed irrelevant. To them, I was just another name on their caseload, another person who might fail.

The system required me to take mental, physical, and medical evaluations. I had to prove my worthiness over and over again. Strangers, people who knew nothing about me, sat across from me, asking personal, probing questions about my past, my health, my mental stability, and my finances. I had to explain my life, my choices, my every thought, just to be considered capable of caring for the boys. Every interview felt like a trial, and I was the defendant, defending my right to love and care for my own family.

But in the midst of all the coldness and bureaucracy, there was a bright spot—a woman who felt like an angel sent from God. She was a DFCS worker, too, but she wasn't like the others. Where most of the caseworkers were all business, detached and distant, she was kind. She didn't look at me with suspicion. Instead, she listened. She tried to ease the burden where she could, offering words of encouragement and understanding. She couldn't change the rules or stop the relentless inspections, but in her presence, I felt seen—not as a case number, but as a person. She was just one worker in a massive system, and she didn't have the power to make any big decisions, but her kindness made a world of difference. In those moments, when everything felt too heavy to bear, her support was a lifeline.

Still, even with her kindness, the system remained a mountain I had to climb. The fear that they could take the boys away at any moment loomed over everything. It was as if no matter what I did, no matter how much I loved them, it was never enough for DFCS. They wanted paperwork. They wanted proof. And no matter how hard I tried, I was never sure that I would be able to provide it in a way that satisfied them.

But I had no choice. I had to endure it. I had to keep going, even when it felt like the system was stacked against me. I had to wake up every morning and face another day of jumping through hoops, all for the sake of these boys who had already lost so much. They were my family. They were worth every ounce of struggle, every sleepless night, every moment of doubt.

At the end of the day, DFCS didn't see the love we were building. They didn't see the small victories— the boys laughing again, feeling safe enough to fall asleep without fear, slowly starting to trust that the world wasn't out to hurt them. They only saw a checklist, a list of requirements, and a man trying to keep up. But I saw something different. I saw two boys beginning to heal, beginning to believe in love again. And no system could take that away from me.

Chapter 11

The Gunshot Incident

Some moments in life sear themselves into your memory so deeply that no amount of time, no amount of healing, can ever erase them. The day my eldest son was shot is one of those moments. I can still feel the grip of the steering wheel in my hands, the oppressive heat of the summer air, and the sound of his fragile voice as he said words that would shatter my heart forever.

It was supposed to be a routine visit, just a simple weekend at my niece's house. Part of the court-ordered DFCS plan to slowly transition the boys back into her care. I didn't want to let them go. Every instinct in my body screamed at me to hold on, to protect them, but I had no choice. DFCS had mandated the visit as part of their process. I was trying to stay optimistic, trying to hope for the best—that maybe my niece was finally in a place where she could care for them again. That maybe, just maybe, this difficult chapter of our lives was coming to a close.

But life has a way of pulling the rug out from under you just when you think you've found solid ground. The sun was setting as we pulled out of her apartment complex. The boys were in the backseat, talking quietly, their small voices mixing with the hum of the car's engine. And then, out of nowhere, a gunshot rang out. At first, it didn't register. My mind struggled to make sense of the sound—it was too surreal, too jarring. But when I heard my son's soft, trembling voice from the backseat, everything around me froze.

"Daddy... my leg popped."

There was a second of disorientation before I turned around, and my whole world shifted. There he was, my little boy, slumped in his car seat, blood soaking through his pant leg, pooling at his feet. A stray bullet had found him—an innocent child caught in the crossfire of a senseless act of violence.

The sight of the blood—so much blood—triggered something primal in me. A mix of terror, fury, and helplessness surged through my veins. My youngest son, strapped into his car seat beside his brother, stared at me with wide, confused eyes, too young to fully grasp what had just happened but old enough to feel the fear radiating off of me. I wanted to scream, to cry, to beg the universe to undo what had just happened, but there was no time for that.

My hands shook as I turned the key, slamming the gas pedal to the floor. There was no time to think, no time to hesitate. I drove faster than I had ever driven in my life, weaving through traffic with reckless abandon, all the while trying to reassure both of my sons that everything was going to be okay. But deep down, I didn't know if it would be. I could feel my eldest son's life slipping away with every drop of blood that soaked into the backseat.

"Hold on, baby. Hold on," I whispered, though I don't know if he could even hear me. His face was pale, his breathing shallow, and I was trying not to break down. I was trying not to lose control of the steering wheel with the tears that blurred my vision. My mind was racing, running through every worst-case scenario, battling the fear that was threatening to consume me.

We reached the hospital, and I carried him inside, his small body limp in my arms. Blood soaked through both of our clothes, and all I could think was, "What if I'm too late? What if he dies in my arms?"

The nurses took him from me, rushing him to the back as I stood there, frozen, covered in my son's blood, helpless. In those moments, everything inside me shattered. I had never felt so powerless, so utterly defeated. The man who was supposed to protect his children, supposed to keep them safe from the evils of the world, had failed.

He was transferred to a children's hospital where he was immediately rushed into surgery. And there I sat, in the cold, sterile waiting room, my parents beside me, my youngest son asleep in their arms, too young to understand the magnitude of what was happening. There was nothing to do but wait. Nothing to do but pray.

The hours dragged on, each one heavier than the last. I kept playing that moment over and over in my mind—the gunshot, the blood, my son's voice whispering, "Daddy, my leg popped." I kept asking myself the same question: "Why him? Why my son?" I felt a crushing sense of guilt, as if there was something I could have done to prevent this, something I had missed. Was there a sign, a moment where I could have stopped the chain of events that led to this?

It's a question I carried for years, long after the doctor came out to tell us that my son had made it through surgery, that he was stable, that he would survive.

Even with the knowledge that he was going to live, the guilt didn't leave me. It latched onto me, clung to me like a shadow. I became obsessed with the idea that I had somehow failed him—that my love hadn't been enough to shield him from the cruelty of the world.

For weeks, I hovered over him like a hawk, watching his every move, listening to every breath. I became the definition of a helicopter dad, unable to let go, unable to stop hovering, terrified that if I looked away for even a second, something else would happen. People started calling me "Helicopter Dad" as a joke, but to me, it wasn't funny. It was survival. I needed to know where they were at every moment, needed to be able to protect them from a world that had already shown me it could take them away in the blink of an eye.

But the guilt… the guilt ate away at me. It gnawed at my heart, my mind. No matter how many people told me it wasn't my fault, no matter how many times I was reminded that I couldn't have predicted or prevented the shooting, I couldn't shake the feeling that I had somehow failed. I was supposed to protect him. I was supposed to be his shield. And I hadn't been.

It took years for me to forgive myself. To accept that I wasn't all-powerful, that I couldn't control everything, no matter how hard I tried. But even now, the memory of that day lingers, a scar on my soul. I still hear gunshots when I close my eyes at night. I still see the blood. I still hear his voice.

And though I've learned to live with the guilt, to push it to the back of my mind, it's always there. A reminder of how fragile life is, how quickly it can be taken away.

In the years that followed, I became more protective of my sons. Maybe too protective at times. But after that day, I knew I couldn't afford to take any chances.

I couldn't afford to let my guard down. Because the world had already shown me what it was capable of. And I wasn't going to let it take or do anything else to us if I could help it.

Chapter 12

The Father I Became—The Father I Lost

It was 2017 when my world began to unravel in ways I never could have imagined. My father, a man who had always seemed larger than life, was diagnosed with cancer. The doctors' prognosis was devastating: three weeks to live. Just three weeks to say goodbye to the man who had been the cornerstone of our family, the man whose presence loomed so large in my life that I couldn't fathom a world without him.

But true to his nature, my father defied the odds. Stubborn, determined, he fought not for just three weeks, but for three grueling months. During those months, we lived in a constant state of turmoil—hope colliding with despair, grief mingling with the fleeting joy of his temporary recoveries. We clung to him, as if by sheer will we could hold on long enough to find some miracle that would make it all go away. It felt like we were living on borrowed time, and every day that passed was a mixture of gratitude for his survival and dread of what was inevitably coming.

My father wasn't just a man. He was a force, the kind of father any boy would have been proud to have. Strong, compassionate, and wise, he didn't just talk about what it meant to be a man—he embodied it. Every decision he made, every sacrifice, every lesson, was infused with love and dedication to our family. Growing up, I watched him lead by example, showing me what it meant to truly care for others, to be responsible, to be honorable. And in those final months, I realized just how much of who I was had been molded by his hands.

But watching him suffer was unbearable. There were days when I sat beside his bed, helpless, as the disease ravaged his once strong body. Our home became a place where the laughter and joy that had once filled the walls were replaced by a heavy silence. My siblings and I exchanged quiet glances, each of us trying to stay strong for our mother, but watching my father fade away was breaking something in each of us that no one, not even our own selves could fix. My mother was with him every moment, her unwavering faith guiding her, but I could see the cracks in her strength, the moments when she'd step out of the room and allow herself to grieve the man she was slowly losing.

The hardest part was knowing we were all helpless. The man who had always been our protector, who had always known what to do, was now the one we couldn't save. There was a heaviness in the air—a collective fear that we tried to keep at bay, even though we all knew the truth. We were losing him, and there was nothing any of us could do.

When we found out that the doctors wanted to send him to a hospice center, my mother refused. She wasn't going to let him die in some sterile, unfamiliar place. If he was going to leave this world, it would be in the comfort of his own home, surrounded by the family he loved so deeply. "If he's going to pass, he's going to pass right here," she said, her voice filled with the quiet determination that had always defined her.

And so, our home became a place of waiting, of watching. But through the sadness, there were moments of beauty. My mother would often sit by his bedside and reminisce about the life they had shared—the early years when he was the sexiest man she had ever seen, the way he'd make her laugh, the way he worked so hard to provide for us, making sure she never had to lift a finger if she didn't want to. She spoke about their life together, the things they had done, and the things they hadn't, wishing they had traveled more, explored more of the world together. But even in her regrets, there was no bitterness—just love. She had loved him completely, and he had loved her the same.

It was a strange kind of love, one that was as fiery as it was tender. They fought sometimes, and when they did, it was intense, but they always found their way back to each other. And even though I sometimes wondered how they could have loved each other so fiercely and yet fought so passionately, I knew their love was real. It was imperfect, but it was theirs. And I admired them for it, even as I told myself I'd want something a little different for myself.

The day I broke down came unexpectedly. I had been holding it together for so long, trying to be strong for my family, for my children, for myself. But one night, as I sat by my father's bedside, watching him struggle for breath, the weight of it all became too much. The pain, the fear, the helplessness—it overwhelmed me, and I found myself sobbing, begging my mother to pray for a miracle.

"Please, Mom," I remember saying, my voice choked with tears. "Please ask God to heal him. We can't lose him. I can't lose him."

My mother, always the pillar of strength, took me by the shoulders and shook me gently. Her eyes, though filled with sadness, held a peace I couldn't understand at the time.

"Baby," she said softly, "I am praying. Just not the way you are. You're praying for God to heal his body, but I'm praying for God to heal his soul."

Her words stopped me cold. I didn't understand what she meant, not fully. How could she be so calm, so accepting, when I was falling apart inside? How could she talk about healing his soul when all I wanted was for him to stay here with us, alive, breathing?

But as the days went on, I began to understand. My mother wasn't giving up. She wasn't abandoning hope. She was simply looking at the situation with a wisdom and faith that I hadn't yet grasped. She knew that my father's time was coming to an end, and she wasn't praying for him to stay in this broken body, suffering and in pain. She was praying for his peace, for his release from the suffering he had endured for so long. She was praying for the healing that comes after life, the healing of the soul.

Those words stayed with me in the days that followed. They were a reminder that, sometimes, the healing we want isn't the healing we need. And as much as it hurt to let my father go, I began to accept that his body was failing, and that maybe— just maybe—my mother was right.

The day my father took his last breath will forever be etched in my soul. The house had been filled with visitors for days, but at that moment, everything became still. There was a silence so profound that it felt like the world had stopped. And in that silence, my mother was the first to speak. "He's gone," she whispered, her voice thick with sorrow but somehow peaceful. "He's back with the Heavenly Father now."

In the quiet that followed, I knew what had to be done. I turned to the room, my voice steady despite the tears threatening to spill over. "Someone grab me a tub," I said. "Fill it with water. Get me some soap and a washcloth."

Although we had cared for my father daily, ensuring he was clean and comfortable as his body failed him, I needed to do this final act of service. I wanted to honor him in the only way I could, to bathe him from head to toe, so that when the funeral home came to take his body, they would be taking the man I knew—clean, dignified, proud.

I bathed him slowly, deliberately. Each stroke of the washcloth a tribute to the man he had been. His body, once so full of life and strength, was now still. But in that final act, I felt closer to him than ever before. It was my way of saying goodbye, of showing him that, even in death, he would be respected, cared for, loved.

The pain of losing him was unbearable, but there was also a strange sense of peace in knowing that he was no longer suffering. His fight was over, and in the

100

stillness of that moment, I felt his presence in a different way—no longer in his body, but in the memories he had left behind, in the lessons he had taught me, and in the legacy of love and strength he had passed down to me.

His death shattered me in ways I can't fully describe, but it also made me stronger. It made me realize that the best way to honor him was to continue living the life he had taught me to live. To be the father, the man, the person he had always believed I could be.

And as the days turned into weeks, and the weeks into months, I carried him with me. Not in the pain of his loss, but in the strength of his memory. I became the father he had taught me to be. The father I had always aspired to be. And though his absence was profound, his presence was felt in every decision I made, in every step I took.

Chapter 13

Holding the Pieces Together

Life after my father's death was like trying to walk through quicksand. We did our best to live as we had before, but his absence left a void that none of us knew how to fill. We tried, of course. We all tried to act as if things were normal, but nothing was normal anymore. The routines we had once taken for granted—the dinners, the conversations, the laughter—all felt hollow. We were just going through the motions pretending to be okay when in reality, we were barely staying afloat.

My older brother, the boys' grandfather, was getting sicker, and the weight of his illness compounded the grief we were already drowning in. My mother, who had always been the rock of our family, was unraveling before my eyes. She was doing her best to take care of my brother, just as she had done for my father, but it was becoming clear that she was breaking under the strain. She was no longer the vibrant, strong woman I had always known. The grief, the stress—it was too much for her to bear.

She stayed in their bedroom most days, her world shrinking down to those four walls. She only left to grab a bite to eat, use the bathroom, or take a bath. It was as if the light inside her had dimmed, and I didn't know how to bring her back. I watched her lose weight, her once-full hair thinning before my eyes, her face drawn and tired. And there was nothing I could do but watch. The mother I had always known—the one who had been there for me in every moment, who had raised me with love and care—was slipping away. And no matter how much I wanted to help; I didn't know how.

It was a strange thing, watching the woman who had always been my caretaker now needing care herself. The roles were reversing, and I wasn't sure I was ready for it. My father had been the protector, the provider, and without him, the weight of that responsibility fell squarely on my shoulders.

I had already taken on the task of raising my two sons, navigating the challenges of single fatherhood, and trying to make ends meet. But when I saw my mother in that state, there was no question in my mind—I had to step up again. There was no other choice. She needed me. My nephew, who had been living with her and my father, needed me too. And I wasn't going to let them down.

I remember sitting in my living room one evening, after tucking the boys into bed, thinking about everything that had happened, everything we had lost. My mind was racing, but one thing was clear—I couldn't let my family fall apart. I had to be the glue that held us together, no matter how much it hurt, no matter how heavy the burden became. I couldn't let my mother suffer alone, couldn't let my nephew grow up in a house filled with so much pain. So, I made a decision that would change everything. I brought my mother and my nephew into my home, where they would be safe, where they would be loved.

It wasn't an easy decision, but it was the only one that made sense. My mother needed care that she wasn't getting, and my nephew needed stability. I was already stretched thin, but love doesn't have limits. I loved them too much to let them continue the path they were on. So, from that day forward, I vowed to take care of them, just as they had taken care of me. I would protect them. I would make sure they were safe.

The transition wasn't easy. My house, once filled with just my two boys and me, now had my mother and nephew under its roof as well. There were adjustments to be made, routines to be shifted, but I didn't mind. I was just grateful that I could do this for them—that I could give them the love and care they deserved.

But there were nights when the weight of it all was almost too much to bear. I would lie awake in bed, staring at the ceiling, wondering how long I could keep it up. The financial strain, the emotional toll—

it was all pressing down on me like a boulder. But then I would hear my mother's voice, weak but grateful, telling me how much she loved me, how proud she was of the man I had become. And that was all the motivation I needed. I couldn't let her down. I couldn't let any of them down.

It was during this time that I realized what it truly meant to be strong. Not the kind of strength that comes from muscles or bravado, but the quiet, unyielding strength that comes from love. The strength that allows you to keep going, even when you feel like you have nothing left to give. The strength that comes from knowing that the people you love are counting on you, and you can't afford to let them down.

I didn't know what the future held, but I knew one thing—I wouldn't let my family fall apart. I would be the strength they needed, the protector they deserved. And though the road ahead was uncertain, I was ready to face it. Because love, in the end, was the only thing that mattered. And I had more than enough of that to go around.

Chapter 14
My Brother's Passing

Losing my brother was like losing a piece of myself. It was as if the universe had decided that my family hadn't suffered enough and kept piling on more grief than we could bear. He had been battling health problems for years, but when he lost his vision, it seemed like the light went out of his life. My brother had always been the strong one—the one who took care of others, who never asked for help, who carried the weight of the world on his shoulders without complaint. But when his sight left him, it broke him in a way I had never seen before.

We tried to care for him at home, to give him the support and love he needed, but it wasn't enough. His health continued to deteriorate, and we had no choice but to place him in a nursing home. It was a decision that weighed heavily on all of us. We didn't want him to feel abandoned, didn't want him to think we had given up on him, but we knew it was the only option.

His medical needs were beyond what we could handle, and the nursing home seemed like the best place for him to get the care he required. But it broke him even more.

My brother, who had always been independent, now found himself relying on others for even the most basic tasks. He hated it. I could see the frustration in his eyes every time I visited him. He hated feeling weak, hated needing help. I tried to be there for him as much as I could, visiting him nearly every day, sitting with him, talking to him, trying to bring some light into the darkness that had become his world.

He was angry—angry at the world, angry at his body for betraying him, angry at himself for not being able to fight back the way he used to. And I couldn't blame him. Watching someone who had always been so strong, so capable, struggle with his own helplessness was one of the hardest things I've ever had to witness.

But it was my mother who suffered the most. She had always been my brother's rock, the one he turned to when life became too much. And now, she couldn't fix this. She couldn't make him better. I watched as the weight of her helplessness pulled her down, piece by piece. She never said it out loud, but I knew she was praying for a miracle—praying that God would somehow restore my brother's sight, his strength, his will to live.

The day he died is one that will stay with me forever. He had been in the hospital for complications from heart surgery. His heart had been weakened by years of dialysis, and though the doctors had done everything they could, the damage was too severe. I had been by his side every day, sitting with my mother in the hospital room, watching as his body grew weaker with each passing hour. But that particular day, I went home to gather more clothes, thinking I would be back in no time. This day felt very cold, not in temperature but within my mind. Feeling emotions I couldn't process. I was rushing,

111

not sure of what all I needed to grab because I didn't want to stay gone very long. I knew I had to hurry to get to the hospital to be by my mother's side.

Then, the phone rang as soon as I was about to walk out of the door to head back.

The hospital called to tell me that my brother had passed. My heart stopped. I couldn't process the words. I stood there in the middle of my living room, clutching the phone, unable to speak, unable to think. My brother—my protector, my confidant, my blood—was gone. Just like that. And I hadn't been there.

The guilt was immediate and suffocating. I had left. I wasn't there when he needed me most. How could I have left? The hospital told me my mother was still there, but they hadn't told her yet. I asked them to wait—to please not tell her until I got there. I needed to be the one to break the news.

When I arrived at the hospital, they had placed her in a separate room, away from his body. I walked in, and she looked up at me with eyes that already knew. Somehow, she knew. "Is your brother okay?" she asked, her voice trembling, her hands clutching at the fabric of her clothing. I couldn't answer. The words stuck in my throat, choked by the weight of what I had to say. How do you tell your mother that her son is dead? How do you shatter someone's world like that?

The silence stretched between us, thick and suffocating, until finally, she spoke again. "He's gone, isn't he?" she whispered, her voice barely audible, as if saying the words would make them real. I nodded, tears streaming down my face. And in that moment, I watched my mother's heart break. There's something indescribably painful about watching someone you love so deeply fall apart. It wasn't just grief—it was devastation. Her son was gone, and no amount of faith, no amount of prayer, could bring him back.

The days that followed were a blur of grief and numbness. My brothers, my sister, my mother—we all tried to hold each other up, but we were drowning in our own sorrow. The house was filled with a heavy, oppressive silence, broken only by the sound of tears. We had lost my father, and now we had lost my brother. It felt like the ground had been ripped out from under us, and we didn't know how to stand anymore.

For my mother, the pain was unbearable. She had lost her husband, and now her son. I watched her decline, both physically and emotionally, in the weeks that followed. She tried to be strong for the rest of us, but I could see the cracks in her façade. I could see how much she was hurting, how much she was struggling to keep it together. And there was nothing I could do to ease her pain.

It was I n those dark days that I realized how much my brother's death had affected me as a father. Watching him suffer, watching him lose everything

114

he had worked so hard to hold onto, made me even more determined to be the father my sons needed. I couldn't protect my brother, couldn't save him from the cruelty of life, but I could be there for my sons. I could be the father they needed, even when the world was falling apart around us.

My brother's death, like my fathers before him, was a reminder that life is fragile. That no matter how strong we think we are, no matter how much we try to protect ourselves and the people we love, there are some things we can't control. But I also learned that love—real, unconditional love—can carry you through even the darkest times. It's what held my family together when everything else seemed to be falling apart. It's what kept us going, even when we didn't know how to move forward.

And as much as I miss my brother, as much as it hurts to know that he's gone, I carry him with me every day. His strength, his resilience, his love for his family— it's all a part of me now. And it's what drives me to be the best father I can be. For my sons. For my family.

Chapter 15

Family Foundations

After my brother's death, our home became both a sanctuary and a reminder of all we had lost. It was never quiet, not with my two sons, my nephew, and my mother all living under one roof. But the noise—the laughter, the arguments, the day-today chaos of life—it was a comfort. It was a reminder that, despite everything, we were still here. We were still together.

My nephew, who had been raised by my parents, was struggling the most. He had always been close to my father and had always respected my brother, and losing them both the way he did, my father due to cancer and my brother due to a weakening body due to dialysis was more than he knew how to handle. He was only a teenager, but he had been forced to grow up quickly, taking on responsibilities that no child his age should have to bear. He wanted to help, to be strong for his grandmother, for me, for the boys. But I could see the weight it was putting on him. He was trying so hard to hold it together, but inside, he was hurting. The burden of grief was too much for him to carry alone, but like my brother and father before him, he didn't want to show it. He didn't want to be a burden to anyone else.

And then there was my mother. She had always been the backbone of our family, the one who held us all together. But after losing my father, and then my brother, something in her changed. She became quieter, more reflective. The grief seemed to weigh her down, stealing the vibrant, loving woman I had always known. There were days when she would sit by the window, staring out at the world, lost in her own thoughts. I knew she was thinking about my father, about my brother, about the life they had built together and the future they would never have. I tried to reach her, tried to comfort her, but there was only so much I could do. Grief is a personal journey, and no one can walk it for you.

118

My two sons were too young to fully understand what was happening, but they could feel the weight of the sadness in the house. They had already experienced so much trauma in their short lives, and now, they were watching their new family fall apart in ways they couldn't quite comprehend. But children are resilient, and they found solace in the small, everyday moments of love and laughter that still managed to exist, even in the midst of our pain.

It wasn't easy. There were days when the grief was too much for any of us to handle. There were days when the weight of everything we had lost threatened to suffocate us. But we found strength in each other. My mother, even in her weakened state, was still the glue that held us all together. She was still a mother, still trying to care for me, for the boys, for my nephew, even when she could barely care for herself.

And my nephew—he stepped up in ways I never expected. He had always been mature for his age, but after my brother's death, he became even more responsible. He helped me with the boys, guiding them through their own struggles while dealing with his own. He was quiet, but strong, and I relied on him more than I ever realized. He became more than just a nephew to me—he became a partner in this journey of survival.

There were nights when we would all sit together at the kitchen table, the weight of the world pressing down on us, but in those moments, we found comfort in knowing that we weren't alone. We were a family—broken, battered, but still standing. And as long as we had each other, we knew we could get through anything.

But the truth was, I was scared. I was scared that I wasn't enough—that I wasn't strong enough, that I wasn't capable enough to hold this family together. I had lost so much already—my father, my brother— and the thought of losing anyone else was unbearable. But every day, I got up. Every day, I kept going. Because I had to. Because my sons needed me. Because my nephew needed me. Because my mother needed me.

I wasn't perfect. I made mistakes. There were days when I lost my temper, when the stress and the grief got the best of me, and I lashed out at the people I loved. There were days when I questioned whether I was doing the right thing, whether I was making the right choices for my family. But through it all, I never stopped loving them. I never stopped fighting for them.

And in the end, that's what mattered most. Not the mistakes, not the moments of doubt, but the love. The love that kept us together, the love that gave us the strength to keep moving forward, even when it felt like the world was falling apart.

Chapter 16

The Pandemic Strikes

The pandemic hit like a tidal wave, washing over everything and everyone without warning. The world seemed to stop overnight, and suddenly, everything we knew—our routines, our sense of security—was stripped away. It wasn't just my family reeling from the shock; it was the entire nation, the entire world. Cities that had once bustled with life fell silent. Streets that were once crowded were deserted. It was as if the world had been placed in an eerie, unrelenting pause.

Millions of families, including mine, were grappling with the unimaginable. For many, their loved ones were taken by the virus, and due to the necessary isolation measures, they couldn't even say goodbye. People were separated from their families at a time when they needed each other the most. Husbands and wives, parents and children, siblings, and friends—distanced by walls of hospitals or even worse, by the fear that a simple hug could mean death. The virus tore through communities, making everyone a potential victim, and turning the act of breathing into a danger. Every day brought new numbers—cases, hospitalizations, deaths— and it was as though the life we had known was crumbling, piece by piece. The fear in the air was thick, and with no clear end in sight, despair gripped everyone in its cold, unforgiving hands.

The emotional toll was heavy, not just for those infected but for everyone. Jobs were lost as businesses shut their doors indefinitely. Dreams were put on hold, and the economy teetered on the edge of collapse. Families who had previously thrived found themselves struggling to put food on the table as unemployment soared. For the first time in recent history, the entire world was united in fear, confusion, and uncertainty. And yet, that unity only seemed to make the isolation worse. There was nowhere to run, no place where the virus hadn't touched, no safe haven where people could escape.

Hospitals were overwhelmed, and the healthcare workers who were once regarded as everyday citizens became soldiers on the frontlines of an invisible war. Doctors and nurses were working impossible hours, many without the proper protective gear, doing everything they could to save lives. But the virus was relentless. Beds filled up faster than hospitals could accommodate, and makeshift morgues had to be built in some areas to house the dead. It was a level of devastation that none of us had ever imagined, and it felt as though the ground was being pulled out from under us.

In the midst of all this chaos, both my mother and I fell ill with COVID-19, and the house that had once been filled with noise and life became a place of quiet desperation. We were fighting our own battle, but so was everyone else. Everywhere you turned, someone was grieving, someone was in fear. The virus became an uninvited guest in homes across the country, attacking not only the body but the spirit as well.

My boys were terrified. They watched as their grandmother, the woman who had been their constant source of love and comfort, grew weaker by the day. My mother, who had already suffered so much loss, was now battling this unseen enemy, and none of us knew if she had the strength to fight it. She was already fragile, both physically and emotionally, after losing my father and my brother. Now, with the virus attacking her body, it felt like the final blow.

The world outside wasn't faring any better. Families were separated, unable to visit their loved ones in hospitals. People died alone, isolated from the people they loved the most. Funerals were held over Zoom or with only a few people allowed to attend, robbing families of the closure they so desperately needed. The death toll kept rising, and with every loss, it felt like a piece of the world's soul was being taken away. And while some people clung to their faith, others found it harder and harder to believe in anything as the virus swept through like a plague.

126

The grocery stores were ravaged by panic buyers. Shelves were emptied of essentials, and the struggle to find basic necessities became a daily reality for many. Masks became our new normal, and the simple act of walking outside became something fraught with anxiety. Would you catch the virus from a neighbor, a passerby, or even just touching a surface? No one knew for sure, and that uncertainty was perhaps the cruelest part of it all.

I, too, was struggling. COVID-19 hit me hard, and there were days when I could barely get out of bed. My body ached, my lungs burned, and every breath felt like a battle. But the worst part wasn't the physical pain—it was the helplessness. I couldn't take care of my mother the way I wanted to, the way she had always taken care of me. I couldn't be there for my boys the way they needed me to be. I was trapped in my own body, watching everything around me fall apart, powerless to stop it.

The boys tried to help in whatever ways they could, but they were just children—scared, confused, and unsure of what was happening. My nephew, who had already taken on so much responsibility after my brother's death, now found himself stepping into the role of caretaker. He was barely old enough to understand what was happening, but he did his best. He would sit in his room, whispering words of comfort that I knew he didn't fully believe. He was trying to be brave, trying to be the strong one, but I could see the fear in his eyes every time he looked at me.

One night, when I was too weak to get out of bed, my nephew went to my mom to check on her. "Grandma, what's wrong? Why are you crying?" he asked, his voice trembling. He wanted to come and wake me so that I could rush to my mother's side. But her voice, weak but steady, murmured, "Let him rest."

Even in her final days, my mother was protecting me. She knew she was dying, but she didn't want me to witness it. She didn't want her last moments to be my final memory of her. She loved me so much that she spared me the pain of watching her take her last breath. It was the ultimate act of love—a mother's love, selfless and enduring, even in the face of death.

The next morning, when I finally mustered the strength to check on her, I found her lifeless body, peacefully with a faint smile on her face. That smile—it was her final gift to me. It was her way of telling me that she was at peace, that she was ready to go. And while I was devastated by her loss, that smile gave me a sense of closure, a sense that she had found the peace she had been searching for since losing my father and my brother.

But the grief was overwhelming. Losing my mother, after everything else we had been through, felt like the final straw. She had been the one who held us all together, the one who had guided me through the hardest moments of my life. And now she was gone, leaving a void in our family that could never be filled. I didn't know how to move forward. I didn't know how to be the father my sons needed, how to be the man my nephew looked up to when I felt so broken inside.

In the days that followed, the house felt emptier than ever. The boys didn't know how to process their grief—they had already lost so much in their young lives, and now they had lost the woman who had been their second mother. My nephew, too, was struggling. He had been so close to my mother, and her death hit him hard. He tried to be strong, tried to hold it together for the sake of the family, but I could see the cracks forming in his armor.

And then there was me. I was grieving not just for my mother, but for the life we had lost—the life we would never get back. I was grieving for my father, for my brother, for the version of myself that had existed before all this pain and loss had reshaped me into someone I barely recognized. There were days when I didn't know if I could keep going when the weight of it all felt like too much to bear.

But in the midst of that darkness, something kept me going. It was my sons. It was my nephew. It was the love that still bound us together, even in the face of so much loss. My mother had taught me that love was stronger than death, stronger than grief, stronger than anything the world could throw at us. And in the days and weeks after her death, I clung to that love with everything I had.

We took care of each other, just as my mother had taken care of us. My sons, my nephew, and I—we found a way to keep moving forward, even when it felt impossible. We found strength in each other, in the memories of the people we had lost, and in the love that still lived on in our hearts. And slowly, day by day, we began to heal.

Chapter 17

Sacrifice in Silence

After my mother's death, the weight of responsibility felt like a mountain on my chest. I had always felt the pressure of being a single father, but now, it was something far greater than I had ever known. It wasn't just about being a father anymore; it was about being the last pillar holding up the entire foundation of our fractured family. My sons, my nephew—they looked to me for everything now. There was no one else left to lean on. And while grief still clung to my soul like a shadow, life, as cruel as it could be, didn't give me the space to fall apart. There was no pause button for the heartbreak.

There were days when I would go through the motions, feeling as though I was walking through a thick fog, not entirely sure of where I was headed. The weight of loss—my father, my mother—was always there, pressing down on me, but I couldn't let it show. The boys still needed to see a rock, someone who would give them the illusion that everything was going to be okay, even when I wasn't sure it ever would be.

Financial stress became an ever-present demon in our lives. This is familiar territory I would say, remembering this type of struggle from when my two sons first came into my life. Bills seemed to pile up faster than I could count. My savings were depleted, leaving me in a state of panic because the constant need to provide for the three boys who were growing faster than I could keep up with was overwhelming. The house we lived in started to feel more like a prison of unpaid bills, overdue notices, and mounting debt. The mortgage was behind, and I was constantly juggling which bills to pay, deciding between keeping the heat on or buying groceries. Every month felt like a gamble, hoping that nothing essential would be cut off or taken away.

The weight of not knowing if we'd have enough food to last through the week gnawed at me every single

134

day. It became an obsession, making sure the boys would never have to experience the pang of hunger. I couldn't bear the thought of their stomachs growling in the middle of the night. I always made sure their plates were full, even if it meant cutting back on my own meals. More often than not, I would go entire days without eating, surviving on a few sips of water and whatever scraps were left. When they'd ask why I wasn't eating, I'd brush it off with a smile, saying I wasn't hungry or that I had already eaten earlier. The lie was small, but necessary—anything to protect them from the truth.

The sacrifices I made were invisible to them. Silent, but constant. Each decision I made, each dollar I spent, each moment I lived was for them. Somewhere along the way, I lost myself in the process. There wasn't room for my own needs, my own desires, or even my own grief. Those parts of me had to be tucked away, kept out of sight, because if I let myself unravel, the entire foundation of our family might crumble. I couldn't afford to be weak. Not now. Not ever.

Every night, I would lie in bed, my body aching with exhaustion but my mind racing with thoughts and fears that refused to let me rest. I'd stare at the ceiling, counting the hours I had left until morning, worrying about how I would keep the lights on, how I would pay the mortgage, how I would make sure the boys had enough. The weight of those worries pressed down on me like a lead blanket, and no matter how hard I tried, I couldn't shake them.

There were nights when I would finally drift off in what seemed like a peaceful sleep, only to be jolted awake by a sudden, inexplicable panic. I would get out of bed, my heart pounding, and quietly tiptoe into the boys' rooms, making sure they were still there, still breathing, still safe. It became a ritual— checking on them every night, not because I thought something was wrong, but because it was the only thing that gave me a sliver of peace. After losing so

136

many loved ones I became afraid that death would somehow return and take what was most precious to me. My sons and my nephew meant everything to me. They were the reason I kept going. They were the reason I pushed through the pain, the fear, the exhaustion. They were the only thing that mattered.

Despite the overwhelming fatigue, I kept moving forward. I had no choice. These three boys were counting on me, and I couldn't let them down. My life had become a series of silent sacrifices—ones they would never see, but ones that were necessary for their survival. I never let them see the cracks, the moments when I thought I couldn't do it anymore. I never let them see the weight I carried. Because they deserved better. They deserved a father who was strong, even when I didn't feel strong at all.

There were times I felt like I was drowning in silence—screaming on the inside while holding it together on the outside. I didn't allow myself to cry, didn't allow myself to break down. I couldn't afford the luxury of grief. My mother had taught me the meaning of resilience, and now I was living it, day by day, even when it hurt.

But there were moments, small, fleeting moments, when the boys would smile at me, when they would laugh, when they would wrap their arms around me and tell me they loved me—and in those moments, I found the strength to keep going. They didn't need to know the full extent of my struggles. They just needed to know I was there for them. Always.

Still, even with all that weight on my shoulders, there was one thing that lingered above it all: the aching loneliness of making sacrifices in silence. It wasn't that I wanted praise or recognition for what I was doing—far from it. But there were days when I wished someone could see the battle I was fighting. Someone who could see beyond the surface and understand the full extent of what I was carrying.

And yet, through it all, I kept moving forward, silently sacrificing, because that's what love is. Love is giving everything you have, even when there's nothing left for yourself. It's holding the weight of the world on your shoulders and still finding a way to smile for the ones who depend on you.

In those quiet moments, when the world seemed so heavy and the sacrifices so endless, I found my purpose. My sacrifices weren't just for survival—they were for love, for the boys who depended on me, for the family I had promised to protect. And in that promise, I found the strength to keep going, no matter how heavy the burden became.

Chapter 18
Redemption in Faith

In the depths of my despair, when it seemed like everything was crumbling around me, I found myself turning back to something I had long abandoned— my faith. It wasn't an immediate return or some sudden moment of clarity. No, it was slow, almost imperceptible at first, like the dawning of a new day that you barely notice until the sun is already in the sky.

For so long, I had been angry—angry at God for taking so much from me. I was angry about the loss of my father, my brother, and now my mother. Angry about the endless challenges and pain that seemed to define my life. I couldn't understand why I was being tested this way. Why me? Why my family? Why my boys? Why my nephew? My prayers during those days were less about faith and more about pleading—pleading for relief, for answers, for an explanation that never came.

It felt as though the walls were closing in on me, with each passing day making it harder to breathe. Nights were filled with sleepless hours, where I lay in the silence of my grief, the only sounds being the shallow breaths of my sons and my nephew as they slept. I would stare at the ceiling, my mind clouded with thoughts of hopelessness, replaying the last few years over and over, wishing I could turn back time, wishing I had the power to undo everything that had gone wrong. But no amount of wishing or praying had seemed to change anything.

But something shifted in the quiet moments when the boys were asleep, and the house was still. In those moments, the weight of the world seemed to press down on me harder, and I could feel the cracks in my armor widening. It was in those moments of complete exhaustion, both physically and mentally, that I began to pray again—not with anger, not with demands, but with surrender.

142

It wasn't an elaborate prayer filled with promises or grand gestures. It was a whispered plea, a quiet conversation with the one thing I had been avoiding God. I asked for strength—not for miracles or to erase the pain—but simply the strength to keep moving, to wake up another day and face the life that was now in front of me. I wasn't asking for everything to be perfect; I was just asking for the courage to keep going, to keep fighting for my boys, to keep showing up for them, even when I didn't think I had anything left to give.

Somewhere in those whispered prayers, I found a sense of peace that I hadn't felt in years. A calmness began to settle within me. The heavy, dark clouds didn't disappear, but the storm wasn't as violent. It felt as though a sliver of light had broken through, and in that light, I started to find hope again.

Faith didn't change my circumstances. It didn't bring my mother back, didn't take away the grief or the financial struggles or the fears that kept me up at night. But it gave me something to hold onto when everything else seemed to be slipping through my fingers. It was the smallest seed of hope, but it was enough to remind me that I wasn't alone in this.

My sons and my nephew began to notice the change in me. My eldest, always the quiet observer, asked me one night as I tucked him into bed, "Are you talking to God again?" His question caught me off guard. For so long, I had kept my faith at arm's length, unsure of what I believed anymore. But in that moment, I realized that he had been watching me, noticing the small shifts in my behavior, sensing that something had changed.

"Yes," I said quietly. "I'm talking to God again."

His face softened as if some unspoken relief washed over him. He didn't say anything after that, but I could see the wheels turning in his mind. He was trying to make sense of what faith meant in a world that had been so cruel to us. He didn't have the words for it yet, but I knew he was starting to understand that faith wasn't about having all the answers. It was about finding the strength to keep going, even when the answers didn't come.

As I began to reconnect with my faith, I found myself wanting to bring the boys along with me on that journey. We started going to church again—not every Sunday, but enough to feel connected to something bigger than ourselves. At first, the boys would sit quietly, fidgeting in the pews, their attention drifting away during the sermons. But over time, I could see that something was resonating with them. They were beginning to understand that faith wasn't about perfection or certainty—it was about hope.

And hope became our anchor. It became the thing that kept us grounded when the world felt like it was spinning out of control. As the months passed, I began to see changes in my boys. They started finding their own ways to connect with God. My youngest would whisper quiet prayers before bed, his voice soft so innocent, while my eldest would ask questions about faith—questions that I didn't always have the answers to. My nephew started to increase his faith, started to pray more, and ask more questions about God and his purpose for his life. So instead of going deeper individually with our conversations with God, we explored it together. We explored conversations about faith and hope, and in those conversations, I saw the power of belief taking root in them.

Faith didn't erase our pain, but it gave us the courage to face it. It didn't fix our problems, but it reminded us that we didn't have to face them alone. In the darkest moments, when the weight of loss felt unbearable, faith was the lifeline that kept us from drowning.

My eldest once told me, "Dad, I think God helps us in ways we can't see. It's like he gives us strength without us knowing it." His words, so simple and yet so profound, brought tears to my eyes. He was right.

146

The strength I had been praying for was already inside me. It had been there all along, growing quietly in the background, waiting for me to recognize it.

The boys began to lean on their faith just as I was rediscovering mine. And in doing so, we began to heal—not completely, not all at once, but slowly, in small, beautiful ways. We began to learn that faith wasn't a shield that protected us from pain, but rather a compass that guided us through it. It gave us direction when everything else felt lost.

We weren't alone. And in the end, that's what mattered most—that no matter how many times life knocked us down, we had something, someone, to turn to. We had our faith. And that faith, fragile as it once was, became the unbreakable bond that held our family together through the hardest times.

Faith was no longer just something I practiced—it became something I lived, breathed, and passed on to my sons and my nephew. It became the foundation upon which we built our lives moving forward, no longer defined by loss, but by the strength we had found in each other and in the belief that no matter what, we were never truly alone.

Chapter 19

A New Beginning

There's a certain kind of peace that comes after you've been through the fire. It's not the carefree peace of someone who's never known hardship. No, it's the kind of peace that's hard-earned, the kind that comes from knowing you've survived the worst that life could throw at you and you're still standing. It's the peace of resilience, of quiet strength, of knowing that no matter what happens next, you'll find a way through it.

That's the kind of peace my family and I began to find in the years that followed my mother's death. Our lives were far from perfect, but they were better. Slowly but surely, we began to heal. My sons, who had once been so scared, so unsure of themselves, began to grow into confident, compassionate young men. They had faced more trauma in their young lives than most people ever would, but they carried that trauma with grace. They didn't let it define them;

they let it shape them into stronger, wiser versions of themselves.

My nephew, too, had grown in ways that filled me with pride. He was no longer the wide-eyed boy I had taken in after my parents' death—he was a young man now, standing at the edge of adulthood, ready to take on the world. He had faced more than his fair share of challenges, but he had come through it all with a heart full of kindness and a mind full of wisdom beyond his years.

We had rebuilt our lives, brick by brick, moment by moment, finding joy in the little things—a shared meal, a family game night, a quiet Sunday afternoon. These were the moments that reminded us that we were still a family, that we still had each other, and that, no matter what, we would always have love.

But rebuilding wasn't easy. There were still challenges—financial struggles that kept me up at night, the lingering grief that crept in when I least

150

expected it, the worries about the future that never seemed to go away. But we faced those challenges together, as a family. And that made all the difference.

One of the hardest lessons I had to learn during those years was to stop waiting for the other shoe to drop. For so long, I had lived in fear of what might come next— what tragedy, what loss, what heartache. It was like I was constantly holding my breath, waiting for the next blow, afraid to let myself believe that things could actually be okay. But slowly, I began to let go of that fear. I began to live in the present, to appreciate the moments of peace and joy without worrying about what might happen tomorrow.

I realized that life would always have its ups and downs, its trials and tribulations. But I had been through the worst of it, and I had come out the other side stronger. I had learned to trust in my own resilience, in my family's ability to weather the storm. And that trust allowed me to finally exhale, to finally let myself believe that we were going to be okay.

The boys were growing up so fast, and with each passing year, I saw more and more of the men they were becoming. They were kind, they were strong, they were compassionate. They had learned the value of family, of love, of perseverance. And I knew that no matter what challenges they faced in the future, they would be able to handle them.

My nephew, too, was finding his way. He had graduated from high school and was starting to explore what he wanted to do with his life. Watching him step into adulthood, with all the strength and wisdom he had gained over the years, filled me with a pride I couldn't put into words. He had been through so much, but he had come out the other side with a heart full of love and a mind full of determination.

As I looked at the future, I saw hope. I saw a future where my boys could grow and thrive, where they could build lives of their own, filled with love, joy, and possibility. I saw a future where we could face whatever came our way, not with fear, but with confidence. Because we had already faced the worst—and we had survived.

For the first time in a long time, I wasn't afraid of what the future held. I was excited. I was ready to see where life would take us next, to see how we would continue to grow and evolve as a family. I knew there would still be challenges, still be moments of doubt and fear, but I also knew that we would face them together. And that was enough.

Chapter 20

The Power of Resilience

Resilience isn't something you're born with. It's something life chisels into you, carving out strength where there was once only fear, courage where there was once only doubt. For my family, resilience became not just a trait we possessed, but the very fabric of who we were.

It didn't happen all at once. Resilience was built over time, piece by piece, through every trial and every setback. It was forged in the moments when we felt like giving up, when the weight of the world seemed too heavy to bear. It was the quiet strength that kept us moving forward, even when everything around us seemed to be falling apart.

For my boys, resilience meant learning to live with the trauma of their past without letting it define them. It meant facing the world with open hearts, even after the world had been so cruel to them. It meant trusting again—trusting me, trusting each other, trusting that the future could be better than the past.

I watched them grow in ways that filled me with awe. My eldest son, once so fragile, had become strong and determined. He still carried the scars of his past, both physical and emotional, but he wore them like badges of honor—proof that he had survived, proof that he had come out the other side. He had a quiet strength about him, the kind of strength that doesn't need to be loud or flashy. It was steady, unwavering. And it was beautiful to witness.

My youngest son, too, had learned resilience in his own way. He had always been the more sensitive one, the one who wore his heart on his sleeve. But even he had found a way to navigate the world with a sense of hope and optimism that I hadn't expected. He had faced his own share of struggles, but he never let them dim his spirit. He was a reminder to all of us that resilience wasn't just about surviving—it was about thriving in spite of everything.

156

And then there was my nephew. He had been through so much. Losing both of his grandparents, watching me take on the role of father to his cousins, stepping into a caretaker role far sooner than he should have had to. But he, too, had grown into a man of strength and wisdom. He didn't complain about the responsibilities life had handed him; he simply accepted them and did what needed to be done. His resilience was quiet, almost invisible to the untrained eye, but I saw it in everything he did. I saw it in the way he helped his younger cousins with their homework, the way he took on chores without being asked, the way he carried himself with a quiet dignity that spoke volumes about the kind of person he was becoming.

But resilience wasn't just about my boys. It was about all of us. It was about the way we had learned to find joy in the little things, even when the big things felt overwhelming. It was about the way we laughed together, even when the world outside our door felt like it was falling apart. It was about the way

157

we held onto each other in the darkest moments, knowing that as long as we had each other, we would be okay.

I think back to the countless nights I lay awake, worrying about the future, wondering how I was going to keep everything together. There were times when the stress of it all felt like too much, when the exhaustion—both physical and emotional—threatened to swallow me whole. But in those moments, I would remind myself of what we had already survived. I would remind myself that we had faced some of the worst things life could throw at us, and we were still standing. We were still here. And that was enough.

Resilience is about more than just surviving the storm—it's about learning to dance in the rain. It's about finding beauty in the struggle, about realizing that even in the midst of hardship, there is still so much to be grateful for. And for us, that gratitude came in the form of each other. We were a family, broken in some ways, but stronger because of it. And in the end, that's what resilience is all about. It's about finding strength in the places you least expect it, about realizing that no matter how hard life gets, you have the power to keep going.

Chapter 21

The Joy in Small Victories

When you've been through as much as we had, you learn to appreciate the small victories. The moments of joy that sneak up on you when you least expect it, the moments of peace that feel like tiny miracles in the midst of chaos. It's those moments that keep you going, that remind you that no matter how hard life gets, there's still so much to be thankful for.

For us, those small victories came in the most unexpected ways. They weren't grand gestures or life-changing events—they were the quiet, everyday moments that made us smile, that made us feel like maybe, just maybe, we were going to be okay.

I think about the first time my eldest son laughed after everything that had happened. It was a real laugh, not the forced, nervous chuckles I had heard so many times before. It was a deep, belly laugh that came out of nowhere, catching me off guard. We were watching a silly cartoon, something that had never really made him laugh before. But for some reason, on that day, it did. And I just sat there, soaking it in, my heart swelling with joy. It wasn't just a laugh—it was a sign that he was healing, that he was finding his way back to the boy he had been before the trauma.

It was a small victory, but it meant everything.

There were other moments, too—moments that might have seemed insignificant to anyone else, but to me, they were monumental. The day my youngest son finally started sleeping through the night without waking up from nightmares. The day my nephew brought home his first paycheck from his part-time job and beamed with pride. The day we paid off a lingering mortgage bill that had been hanging over our heads for months. These were the moments that kept us moving forward, the moments that reminded us that we were making progress, even when it didn't always feel like it.

162

I remember the night we all sat around the dinner table, laughing, and joking, just like any other family. It wasn't a special occasion—just an ordinary weeknight. But in that moment, I realized how far we had come. We had been through so much, but we were still here, still laughing, still finding joy in each other's company. And that, to me, was the greatest victory of all.

The small victories added up over time. They became the foundation on which we rebuilt our lives. They reminded us that life wasn't just about the big, life-changing events—it was about the little moments of happiness that we often overlook. It was about the way my sons' eyes lit up when they saw me after a long day at work. It was about the way my nephew would quietly take over household chores when he saw I was too tired to do them. It was about the way we all came together, even in the smallest ways, to support each other.

Those moments may not have seemed like much to anyone else, but to us, they were everything. They were the proof that we were healing, that we were growing, that we were finding our way back to each other. They were the moments that made all the struggles worth it.

I learned to stop waiting for the big, dramatic victories and to start celebrating the small ones. I learned to appreciate the way my boys would wrap their arms around me at the end of a long day, the way we would all pile onto the couch to watch a movie, the way we could make each other laugh, even when things were hard. Those were the moments that reminded me that we were still a family, that we were still capable of love and joy, no matter what life threw at us.

The small victories taught me that happiness isn't something you wait for—it's something you create, every single day, in the way you choose to live your life. It's in the way you show up for the people you love, in the way you find joy in the little things, in the way you keep moving forward, even when the road ahead seems uncertain.

And as time went on, those small victories became the building blocks of our new life. They became the reminders that we were capable of more than we ever thought possible. They became the proof that, no matter how hard things got, we would always find our way back to each other.

Chapter 22

Embracing Imperfection

For years, I believed that being a good father meant being perfect. I thought that I had to have all the answers, that I had to be strong all the time, that I couldn't afford to make mistakes. But as time went on, I realized that perfection was a myth—a dangerous one. The more I chased it, the more I lost sight of what really mattered.

It took me a long time to come to terms with my own imperfections, to accept that I couldn't always be the rock my family needed. There were days when I made mistakes, when the stress and exhaustion got the better of me, and I snapped at my boys or withdrew into myself. I wasn't always the calm, patient father I wanted to be. There were times when I raised my voice, when I lost my temper, when I felt like I was failing them in every possible way.

I remember one night in particular. It had been a long day at work, and when I got home, the house was a mess. The boys were bickering over something trivial, my nephew was distant, and I felt the weight of everything closing in on me. I yelled— something I tried never to do—but in that moment, I couldn't stop myself. The boys fell silent, their wide eyes looking up at me with a mixture of surprise and fear, and the guilt hit me like a tidal wave.

I had failed them. Again.

Later that night, after everyone had gone to bed, I sat alone in the living room, staring at the ceiling, wondering how I could have let things get so out of control. How could I have let my frustration spill over onto them? They didn't deserve that. They deserved better. And in that moment, I felt like I wasn't enough—that no matter how hard I tried, I was never going to be the father they needed me to be.

168

But as the night wore on, I began to realize something. Perfection wasn't the goal—showing up was. Being there, day after day, no matter how tired, no matter how stressed, no matter how many mistakes I made—that was what mattered. It wasn't about being the perfect father; it was about being the father they needed in the moment, even if I stumbled along the way.

The next morning, I sat down with my boys and apologized. I told them that I had made a mistake, that I shouldn't have raised my voice, that I was sorry. They looked up at me with their innocent eyes, and I could see the understanding in their faces. They didn't need me to be perfect. They just needed me to be there.

That was the moment I realized that being a good father wasn't about never making mistakes—it was about admitting when you did. It was about showing them that it was okay to be human, that it was okay to fall short sometimes, as long as you owned up to it and tried to do better.

My boys didn't need a flawless father. They needed a father who loved them enough to admit when he was wrong, who loved them enough to keep trying, even when things were hard. They needed to see that I was doing my best, even when my best wasn't perfect. And that's what I gave them—my best, flaws, and all.

Over time, I learned to embrace my imperfections as a father. I learned that making mistakes didn't make me a bad parent—it made me a real one. I wasn't perfect, but I was present. I was there for my boys when they needed me, even on the days when I felt like I had nothing left to give. I was there when they were scared, when they were sad, when they were happy. I was there through it all.

And in embracing my own imperfections, I taught my boys to do the same. I taught them that it was okay to make mistakes, that it was okay to be vulnerable, that it was okay to ask for help when they needed it. I showed them that strength wasn't about never falling—it was about getting back up, time and time again.

I think back to all the moments when I felt like I was failing them—when the weight of single fatherhood felt too heavy, when the grief, stress, and exhaustion threatened to overwhelm me. But through it all, I never gave up. I kept showing up, day after day, even when it felt impossible. And in the end, that's what made the difference.

Being a father isn't about being perfect. It's about being there, through the good days and the bad, through the triumphs and the mistakes. It's about loving your children with everything you have, even when you feel like you're falling short. And in that love, in that commitment to showing up no matter what, you find the strength to keep going.

My boys didn't need perfection. They needed me—flaws, mistakes, and all. And in the end, that's what I gave them.

Chapter 23

Finding Purpose

As the years went by, and the boys grew older, I found myself thinking more and more about the future—not just theirs, but mine. For so long, my entire identity had been wrapped up in being a father. It was the role that had defined me, that had given my life meaning. But now, as my sons began to find their own way in the world, I started to wonder: Who was I, beyond being their dad?

It was a strange feeling, this sense of uncertainty about my own identity. I had spent so many years focused on raising my boys, on keeping our family together, on surviving the chaos and trauma that had shaped our lives. But now, for the first time in a long time, I had the space to think about what I wanted for myself. What was my purpose, beyond fatherhood? What did I want to do with the rest of my life?

It wasn't an easy question to answer. For years, I had put my own needs and desires on the back burner, always prioritizing my sons, always focusing on their well-being. But now, as they grew older and more independent, I realized that I had a chance to rediscover myself, to find a new sense of purpose that went beyond my role as a father.

I started to think about all the other single parents out there, especially the single fathers who, like me, had been thrust into this role without much warning or preparation. I thought about how isolating it could be, how overwhelming the responsibility felt, and how many times I had wished for someone to talk to, someone who understood what I was going through.

That's when I realized that my purpose wasn't just about my boys—it was about helping others who were walking the same path. I had been through so much, learned so many hard lessons along the way, and I felt a deep need to share those experiences with others. I wanted to be a voice of hope and encouragement for other single parents who might be struggling, just as I had.

So, I began to speak. I started sharing my story with others—at local community centers, at support groups for single parents, even at church. At first, it felt strange, standing in front of a room full of strangers and baring my soul. But the more I spoke, the more I realized how much my story resonated with others. I wasn't the only one who had faced these challenges. I wasn't the only one who had felt lost, scared, and overwhelmed.

I met other single parents who were going through the same struggles—financial difficulties, emotional exhaustion, the constant fear of not being enough for their children. And as we shared our stories, I saw the power of connection, the power of knowing that you're not alone. I saw the relief in their faces, the way their shoulders relaxed just a little when they realized that someone else understood.

In sharing my story, I found a new sense of purpose. I realized that everything I had been through—every hardship, every challenge, every sleepless night—had prepared me to help others. It had given me the strength and the wisdom to offer support to those who needed it most. And in helping others, I found healing for myself.

I also began writing, documenting my journey as a single father, sharing the lessons I had learned along the way. Writing became a way for me to process everything I had been through, to make sense of the chaos and find meaning in the pain. And as I wrote, I realized that my story wasn't just about survival—it was about resilience, about love, about the power of family to heal even the deepest wounds.

My purpose became clear: I was here to help others, to offer hope and encouragement to those who felt like they couldn't keep going. I was here to remind them that, no matter how hard things got, they were capable of more than they ever imagined. I was here to show them that love—real, unconditional love—was the most powerful force in the world, and that it could carry them through even the darkest of times.

Finding my purpose didn't mean that everything became easy. There were still challenges, still moments of doubt and fear. But now, I had a sense of direction, a sense of meaning that went beyond just getting through the day. I knew that my experiences mattered, that my story had the power to help others. And that gave me the strength to keep going.

In the end, finding purpose wasn't about discovering something new—it was about recognizing the value of what I had already been through. It was about understanding that my journey, with all its pain and struggle, had prepared me for something greater. And as I embraced that purpose, I found a sense of peace that I hadn't known before.

Chapter 24

A Future Filled with Hope

As I sit here, reflecting on the journey we've been through, I can't help but feel an overwhelming sense of hope. It's not the kind of naïve hope that comes from believing everything will be perfect. It's the kind of hope that's been tested in fire, the kind that's stronger because of the trials it's endured.

Life isn't perfect—far from it. There are still days when I worry about the future, when the weight of responsibility feels heavy on my shoulders. But there's also peace in knowing that we've survived so much already. We've faced some of the hardest challenges life could throw at us, and yet, here we are—still standing, still moving forward, still together.

My sons are growing up so fast, and every day, I see them becoming more and more of the men they were always meant to be. They are strong, kind, resilient young men who have faced more than most people will in a lifetime, and yet they carry themselves with grace and compassion. They've learned what it means to persevere, what it means to love unconditionally, and what it means to find joy even during hardship.

My eldest, once so fragile, and fearful, has become a pillar of quiet strength. He doesn't let the world see his scars, but I know they're there—both the visible ones and the ones hidden deep inside. He's learned to live with them, to carry them as part of his story, but not to let them define him. He's grown into a young man I couldn't be prouder of, and I know that whatever life throws at him, he will face it with the same courage and resilience he's shown throughout his life.

My youngest son, too, has blossomed into someone who radiates warmth and optimism. His heart is still wide open, despite everything he's been through, and that's something I admire so much about him. He hasn't let the pain of his past harden him; instead, he's used it to grow into someone who spreads kindness wherever he goes. He's the kind of person who makes the world a better place just by being in it, and I know he will do great things.

And then there's my nephew—no longer the boy I once took in, but a man standing at the threshold of his future. He's wise beyond his years, shaped by the losses we've endured and the responsibilities he took on far too young. But he's never let those things break him. Instead, they've molded him into someone I admire deeply. He's strong, thoughtful, and compassionate, and I know that whatever path he chooses in life, he will walk it with grace and purpose.

The house we live in today is filled with love. It's not perfect—there are still challenges, still moments of grief that catch us off guard, still worries about what the future might hold. But there's also laughter. There's joy. There's a deep, unshakable sense of togetherness that I know will carry us through whatever comes next.

For the first time in a long time, I'm not afraid of what the future holds. I'm excited. I look at my sons, at my nephew, and I see all the possibilities ahead of them. I see a future where they can grow, where they can build lives of their own, where they can love deeply and be loved in return. I see a future where they can pursue their dreams, unburdened by the trauma of their past, but strengthened by the resilience they've gained from it.

I know there will still be challenges. Life has a way of throwing curveballs when you least expect it. But I also know that we've built something strong—something that can withstand whatever comes our way. We've learned how to bend without breaking, how to rise after every fall, how to love through every storm.

As I look ahead, I see hope. I see love. I see resilience. And I know that whatever the future holds, we'll face it together.

Conclusion

The Power of Love

If there's one thing this journey has taught me, it's that love—real, unconditional love—is the most powerful force in the world. It's not the kind of love that comes easily, the kind that's all roses and sunshine. It's the kind of love that shows up when everything is falling apart, the kind that stays when it would be easier to leave. It's the kind of love that holds you together when you're too tired, too broken, too scared to keep going.

That love is what carried me through the hardest moments of my life. It's what kept me going when I didn't think I had anything left to give. It's what made me get out of bed every morning, even when the weight of grief and fear felt unbearable. It's what gave me the strength to keep fighting for my sons, for my nephew, for our family.

I think back to my father—the man who first showed me what it meant to love unconditionally. He wasn't perfect, but he was steadfast. He loved us with everything he had, even when life threw challenges his way. And it was his love, his unwavering commitment to our family, that laid the foundation for the kind of father I would one day become.

When I lost him, I felt like a piece of myself was ripped away. I didn't know how to move forward without him. But over time, I realized that his love hadn't left me. It was still there, guiding me, shaping me, helping me become the man I needed to be for my sons. His love became my anchor, my guiding light, even in his absence.

And then there was my mother—strong, wise, and filled with a quiet, unwavering faith. She taught me that love wasn't just about fixing things; sometimes, it was about simply being there. It was about holding space for the people you love, even when you couldn't take their pain away. She showed me that love could be gentle and fierce at the same time, that it could heal even the deepest wounds.

When I became a father, I didn't know if I could live up to the example my parents had set. I didn't know if I was strong enough, patient enough, wise enough to be the father my boys needed. But what I've learned is that fatherhood isn't about being perfect. It's about showing up, day after day, no matter how hard it gets. It's about loving your children with everything you have, even when you don't have all the answers.

This journey has been filled with more pain and heartache than I ever could have imagined. But it's also been filled with more love than I ever thought possible. Love that endured through every trial, every setback, every moment of doubt. Love that held us together when everything else seemed to be falling apart.

In the end, it wasn't the challenges that defined our story—it was the love we found during them. The love that gave us the strength to keep going. The love that reminded us that no matter how hard life got, we were never alone.

If there's one thing I hope you take away from this story, it's this: Love is enough. It's enough to carry you through the darkest nights, enough to heal the deepest wounds, enough to bring you back to life when everything else feels like it's crumbling. Love is what will save you. It's what will save us all.

Letter From My 10-Year-Old Son

Dear Dad,

Thank you for being the best dad ever. You always take care of us and make sure we're safe. I know you do a lot for me and my brother, and I just want to say that I love you so much. You always help me when I'm scared, and you always make me feel better when I'm sad.

Even though things are hard sometimes, you make everything better just by being there. Thank you for playing with us and for teaching us new things. I'm really lucky to have a dad like you.

Love,
Nickolus

Letter From My 12-Year-Old Son

Dear Dad,

I just want to say thank you for everything you do for us. I know that being a dad is hard sometimes, but you always make sure we have what we need. You take care of us no matter what, and I'm really thankful for that.

There are so many things you do that show how much you love us—like when you help us with homework or make sure we have food to eat even when things are tough. You always look out for me and my brother, and I know you work hard so that we can have a good life.

Thank you for always being there and for teaching me how to be strong. I hope one day I can be as great as you are.

Love,
Demetrise

Letter From My 18-Year-Old Nephew

Dear Uncle,

I don't even know where to begin to say thank you. You've been more than an uncle—you've been a father to me in every way that matters. You stepped up when I needed you the most, and I'll never forget that.

I know these past few years haven't been easy for any of us, but you always held things together, even when it seemed like everything was falling apart. You've taught me so much—about being strong, about working hard, about love and family. You showed me that even in the hardest times, we can find a way to keep going.

I look up to you in so many ways, and I hope that as I move into adulthood, I can carry the lessons you've taught me forward. You've given me more than I could ever repay, and I'm so grateful for everything you've done for me and for my cousins.

Thank you for believing in me and for always being there. I love you, and I'm proud to call you not just my uncle, but my dad.

Sincerely,
Jaquavious

A Letter of Gratitude

To My Sons and My Nephew

There aren't enough words to fully express how grateful I am for each of you. You've given me a gift that is beyond measure—the gift of being your father. From the moment you entered my life, you changed everything. You filled my days with purpose, my heart with love, and my spirit with strength.

To my sons, you came to me when you were just little boys, unsure of the world and everything in it. Together, we've walked through some of the hardest times, but through it all, you've shown me what resilience looks like. You've grown into such incredible young men, filled with kindness, courage, and wisdom beyond your years. You've made me laugh, you've made me proud, and most of all, you've made me better. Thank you for teaching me about unconditional love, for allowing me to be your father, and for making every sacrifice worth it. I love you both more than words can say.

To my nephew, I'm so proud of the man you've become. You've faced trials that most your age never have to, but you've come through them with grace and strength. You've not only been a son to me, but also a big brother to your cousins. Your heart is full of love, and your character is full of integrity. I'm grateful for every moment we've shared, for the way you've stepped up for this family, and for the way you've grown into a young man that anyone would be proud to call their own. Thank you for being by my side through it all, for being a part of this family, and for making me proud every single day.

A Note to Myself
To myself—I want to take a moment to acknowledge all that I've done. I've carried the weight of fatherhood, the weight of loss, and the weight of countless sacrifices on my shoulders, and I'm still standing. I've been through some of the darkest moments, but I've never let them defeat me. I've provided for my family, protected them, loved them fiercely, and held them close, even when the world seemed too heavy to bear.

I'm proud of myself for the growth I've gone through, for the times I've chosen to keep going even when it felt impossible. I've learned to love without reservation, to sacrifice without expectation, and to lead my family with both strength and vulnerability. I've grown in ways I never expected, and I've come through this journey stronger than I ever imagined I could be.

So, to myself, I say: I'm proud of you. I'm proud of the father you've become, the man you've become, and the way you've never given up. You've done what many thought impossible, and you did it with love.

To My Parents
Mom and Dad, you were the ones who first showed me what love, family, and sacrifice truly mean. The

193

lessons you taught me shaped the man and father I've become today. Dad, you taught me what it means to be strong, to love with everything you have, and to never back down from responsibility. Mom, your unwavering faith, and love have been my guide through life's most difficult moments. You both gave me the foundation that carried me through fatherhood, and I'm forever grateful for everything you instilled in me. Thank you for your love, your wisdom, and your sacrifices. I carry your teachings with me every day.

Most Importantly to God
God, without You, none of this would have been possible. Through every trial, every moment of doubt, you were my strength. When I didn't think I could keep going, you lifted me up. You gave me the grace to endure the losses, the courage to face the unknown, and the faith to trust that things would get better, even when I couldn't see the way. You brought my sons and my nephew into my life for a
reason, and for that, I am eternally thankful. Thank You for guiding me, for never letting me fall, and for filling my heart with love and resilience. I owe everything to You.

With all my love and gratitude,
Christopher Cornelius Walls

Navigating the Storm of Grief

Grief is an ocean, vast and unpredictable. Some days, it feels like you're standing on the shore, watching the waves crash gently in the distance. Other days, the waves are so high and so powerful that they knock you off your feet, leaving you gasping for air, trying to find solid ground. There is no perfect way to handle grief, no step-by-step guide that will tell you how to get through it unscathed. It's a journey, a personal experience that is different for everyone. But if there's one thing I've learned, it's that grief is not something you "get over." It's something you learn to carry, something you learn to live with.

The first thing to understand about grief is that it is not linear. It doesn't move in a straight line or follow a predictable path. There are stages, yes—denial, anger, bargaining, depression, and acceptance—but they don't happen in order, and they don't always happen neatly. One day, you may feel like you're moving toward acceptance, only to be hit with a wave of anger or sadness the next. This is normal. This is grief.

In the aftermath of loss, it's easy to feel like you should "be better" or "move on" after a certain amount of time. But the truth is, there is no timeline for grief. Whether it's been days, months, or years, the pain of losing someone you love can resurface when you least expect it. And that's okay. Grief is a reflection of love, and when you love someone

195

deeply, it's only natural that the loss of them will impact you deeply as well.

So, how do you handle grief? How do you manage the waves when they feel like they're threatening to drown you? The answer, I've found, lies in accepting that grief is not something you conquer—it's something you learn to navigate. And there are tools and practices that can help you stay afloat, even on the darkest days.

Allow Yourself to Feel

One of the most important things to remember about grief is that it's okay to feel. It's okay to cry. It's okay to be angry, to feel lost, to feel confused. Too often, we try to suppress our emotions, thinking that if we push them down deep enough, they'll go away. But that's not how grief works. In fact, the more you try to ignore it, the more it will find its way back into your life, sometimes when you least expect it.

Allow yourself to feel whatever it is you're feeling. Give yourself permission to be sad, to miss the person you lost, to wish things were different. Grief is messy, and it's okay to not have it all together. There will be days when you feel like you're making progress, and there will be days when it feels like you're back at square one. Both are part of the process.

196

Seek Therapy and Counseling

Grief is heavy, and sometimes it's too heavy to carry on your own. That's where therapy and counseling come in. There is no shame in seeking help. Talking to a professional—someone who is trained to help you process your emotions—can make a world of difference. Therapy gives you a safe space to talk about your grief, to explore the emotions you might be too afraid to voice out loud to friends or family. It provides a non-judgmental environment where you can say what you're truly feeling, without the fear of burdening others.

Counselors and therapists can offer you tools to help manage your grief. Whether it's learning how to reframe certain thoughts, finding healthy ways to express your emotions, or simply having someone to listen to you, therapy can be an invaluable resource during the grieving process.

Group therapy is another option that some find helpful. There's something incredibly comforting about being in a room full of people who know exactly what you're going through. Grief can feel isolating, like you're the only person in the world feeling this kind of pain. But group therapy reminds you that you're not alone. You hear stories of others who have faced similar losses, and in those shared experiences, you find strength, solidarity, and hope.

Turning to God and Faith

For me, faith has been one of the most powerful tools in navigating grief. It's easy to lose faith in the wake of loss, to question why God would allow something so painful to happen. I've been there. I've wrestled with those questions. But what I've come to realize is that faith doesn't take away the pain, but it gives us the strength to endure it.

Having a prayer life and a higher spiritual awareness can bring peace in the midst of chaos. Prayer isn't about asking for the pain to go away; it's about finding the strength to keep going, even when the pain is overwhelming. When you pray, you're not alone in your grief. You're speaking to someone who understands the depth of your pain, someone who has the power to provide comfort in ways that are beyond our understanding.

Grief has a way of shaking your faith, but it can also deepen it. In those moments of raw vulnerability, when you have nothing left to give, turning to God can remind you that you don't have to carry it all on your own. The Bible speaks of God being close to the brokenhearted, of His promise to never leave us nor forsake us. These are not just words—they are truths to hold onto when everything else feels unstable.

Sometimes, it's in the darkest moments of grief that we find our faith renewed. We remember that God is not just a distant being, but a present help in times of trouble. And while faith doesn't erase the grief, it

198

gives us a sense of hope—a hope that even in the pain, there is a greater plan, a greater purpose, one that we may not fully understand but one that we trust is being worked out.

Finding Support

Don't be afraid to lean on others. Grief can make you feel like you need to carry the burden alone, but that's not true. Whether it's family, friends, or a support group, reach out to those around you. Let them be there for you. It's okay to ask for help, to say that you're struggling. The people who love you want to support you—they just might not know how unless you tell them.

Sometimes, just talking to someone who listens, who lets you vent without offering solutions, can make a world of difference. Surround yourself with those who uplift you, who remind you of the love and light that still exists, even when it feels overshadowed by loss.

Remembering and Honoring Your Loved One

Grief doesn't mean forgetting. One of the most important things I've learned is that it's okay to continue loving and remembering the person you lost. Create rituals that allow you to honor their memory, whether it's lighting a candle, visiting their resting place, or simply talking about them with family and friends. Keeping their memory alive doesn't keep you stuck in grief—it helps you find a

199

way to carry their love with you as you move forward.

Walking Through the Valley

Remember, grief is one of life's greatest challenges, but it's also one of the ways we learn to grow, to love deeper, and to appreciate the precious moments we have with the people still in our lives. It's a journey with no end date, but with time, the waves that once knocked you off your feet become smaller. You learn to navigate the waters, to find peace in the midst of the storm. And with faith, therapy, and the love of those around you, you find a way to live again—not as you did before, but with a deeper understanding of the fragility and beauty of life.

Dating Advice for Single Parents

Dating as a single parent is a unique challenge—one that requires patience, honesty, and a deep understanding of your priorities. The world of dating, already complex, takes on new layers when you have children to consider. Every decision, every potential relationship, must be weighed not just in terms of your own desires, but in terms of how it will affect your children.

For me, the decision to start dating again came after years of focusing solely on my sons and my nephew. I had spent so much time making sure they were okay, making sure our family was stable, that I hadn't allowed myself to even think about what I needed. But as they grew older, I realized that it was okay to want something for myself, too.

The first thing I learned about dating as a single parent is that timing is everything. It's important to make sure that you and your children are in a place of stability before bringing someone new into your lives. My sons had already been through so much upheaval—I knew that if I was going to introduce someone new into their lives, it had to be the right person at the right time.

When I eventually did start dating again, I approached it with caution. I was upfront with anyone I dated about my situation. My children came first—always. And if someone wasn't okay with that, it wasn't going to work. It's important to set those boundaries early on, to be honest about your responsibilities as a parent. Not everyone will be willing or able to take on the complexities that come with dating a single parent, and that's okay. It's better to know that upfront than to get emotionally involved with someone who can't handle it.

One of the hardest parts about dating as a single parent is guilt. I often felt like I was being selfish, like I was taking time away from my sons to pursue something that was just for me. But what I eventually realized was that it wasn't selfish at all. Taking care of myself—my own emotional and mental well-being—was just as important as taking care of them. They needed me to be happy, to be fulfilled, to be whole. And part of that meant allowing myself to seek companionship and love.

Financial Advice for Single Parents

Navigating the financial landscape as a single parent is one of the most challenging aspects of raising a family alone. Every decision, every dollar, and every moment spent budgeting can feel overwhelming at times, especially when the stakes are high, and you're responsible for more than just yourself. Over the years, I've learned a few strategies that helped me keep my family afloat, even when the financial waters were rough.

1. Create a Budget and Stick to It

The first, and perhaps most important, step in managing your finances as a single parent is creating a budget. This isn't just a loose plan for how you'll spend your money—it's a detailed, realistic blueprint for how you'll make ends meet each month. When I first became a single father, I quickly realized that the way I had been managing my finances as an individual no longer worked for a household of four.

I sat down with a notepad and wrote down every single expense I had, from the big ones like rent and utilities, to the smaller ones like school supplies and snacks for the boys. It was eye-opening to see how quickly the little things added up. From there, I looked at my income and figured out where I could make adjustments. It meant cutting out luxuries— cable, dining out, and even little indulgences like coffee runs.

Sticking to that budget was hard, especially at first. There were months when unexpected expenses would throw everything off course—a car repair, a medical bill—but having that budget gave me a sense of control. It helped me prioritize the essentials: shelter, food, utilities, and transportation. Everything else had to be secondary.

2. Build an Emergency Fund (Even If It's Small)

One of the lessons I learned early on was the importance of having an emergency fund. It didn't need to be large—at first, it wasn't even close to covering three months of living expenses—but having something set aside for the unexpected was crucial. Life as a single parent is unpredictable. Whether it's a medical emergency, a broken appliance, or a sudden job loss, having a small safety net can make all the difference.

I started by setting aside a little money from each paycheck. Some weeks, it was only $5, but over time, it added up. The goal is to build up enough to cover at least three months of living expenses, but if that feels overwhelming, start smaller. Even a few hundred dollars can provide a buffer in case of an emergency. The peace of mind that comes from knowing you have something set aside, no matter how small, can alleviate a lot of stress.

3. Tap into Community Resources

One of the things that made a huge difference for my family was learning about the resources available to us. Many cities and towns offer programs for single parents, including food assistance, childcare subsidies, and free or low-cost health services. There's no shame in asking for help when you need it. These programs exist to support families like ours, and they can provide a much-needed lifeline during tough times.

In addition to government assistance, many nonprofit organizations offer support for single parents. Whether it's through financial aid, job training programs, or even counseling services, there are resources out there designed to help ease the burden. I relied on some of these resources myself during particularly difficult periods, and they were instrumental in helping me keep things together.

4. Plan for the Future (Even When It Feels Impossible)

When you're just trying to get through the day-to-day challenges of single parenthood, planning for the future can feel impossible. But it's important to start thinking about long-term financial goals, even if it seems overwhelming at first. One of the best things you can do is start saving for your children's education, even if it's just a little bit at a time.

I opened a college savings account for my boys as soon as I could. At first, I could only contribute a small amount each month—sometimes it was only $20—but over time, that money added up. It's easy to feel like you're not doing enough, but every dollar you save for their future is a step in the right direction.

It's also important to think about your own financial future. Retirement may feel like a distant concern, but it's never too early to start planning. If your job offers a retirement plan, especially one with an employer match, take advantage of it. Even small contributions now can grow over time and provide security later on.

5. Teach Your Children About Money

One of the most valuable things I've done as a single parent is teaching my boys about money. I wanted them to understand the importance of budgeting, saving, and making wise financial decisions from a young age. This wasn't just about teaching them to be financially responsible adults—it was also about involving them in the process, so they understood why certain sacrifices were necessary.

When they were old enough, I started giving them small allowances in exchange for helping around the house. I encouraged them to save a portion of that money, and when they wanted something special—like a toy or a game—I helped them plan how they could save for it themselves. It was a small way to

206

teach them the value of money, and it also helped them understand why we couldn't always afford everything they wanted.

By involving your children in these conversations, you're setting them up for financial success in the future. You're giving them the tools they need to make smart decisions, and you're teaching them that money is something to be managed, not something to be feared.

Adoption Process and Checklist

Adopting my sons was one of the most emotionally intense and rewarding experiences of my life. The process was long, filled with moments of uncertainty, and more than a few sleepless nights. But looking back now, every challenge we faced along the way was worth it. If you're considering adoption or are currently navigating the process, here are some things to keep in mind, along with a checklist to guide you through.

1. Research Your Options

The first step in the adoption process is deciding which type of adoption is right for you and your family. There are several paths to adoption, each with its own set of challenges and rewards:

- Foster Care Adoption: This involves adopting children who are currently in the foster care system. Many of these children have experienced trauma or instability, and adopting from foster care often comes with the added complexity of navigating birth parent rights and reunification processes. However, it's also an opportunity to provide a loving home for a child who truly needs it.

- Private Domestic Adoption: In this scenario, you work directly with an adoption agency or attorney to adopt a child within your own country, often from birth. This process can be quicker than foster care adoption but tends to be more expensive.

• International Adoption: This involves adopting a child from another country, which comes with its own set of legal and logistical hurdles. International adoption can be rewarding but also presents challenges related to cultural adjustment and the legal complexities of cross-border adoption.

2. Understand the Legal and Emotional Complexities

Each type of adoption comes with its own legal requirements and emotional challenges. For domestic or foster care adoptions, you'll need to undergo home studies, background checks, and medical evaluations. The legal requirements may vary by state, so it's crucial to consult with an attorney or agency familiar with adoption laws in your area.

Beyond the legal process, there's an emotional aspect to consider. Adoption is a life-changing decision for both you and the child. Many children in foster care have experienced significant trauma, and even private or international adoptions can involve emotional hurdles for the adoptive parent and the child. Be prepared for a journey that will challenge your heart and mind in unexpected ways.

3. The Home Study Process

One of the most important steps in the adoption process is the home study. During this process, a social worker will visit your home to assess whether it's a safe and supportive environment for a child. This isn't just about whether your home is clean and well-maintained—it's about your ability to provide emotional, financial, and physical stability.

During our home study, the social worker looked into every corner of our lives— literally and figuratively. They opened every drawer, checked the contents of our refrigerator, took note of the boys' sleeping arrangements, and even asked about our routines. It felt invasive at times, and I remember feeling like I was constantly under a microscope. But I also knew that this process was important. The social workers weren't just checking to see if my home was suitable; they were ensuring that my boys would be safe and cared for.

4. Prepare for the Emotional Rollercoaster

Adoption is filled with emotional highs and lows. There will be moments of intense joy and moments of doubt. There will be paperwork delays, emotional setbacks, and moments when the process feels like it will never end. It's important to be patient, to trust the process, and to lean on your support system during the difficult times.

For me, the hardest part was the uncertainty. There were moments when I didn't know if the adoption would go through, moments when I feared that my boys would be taken away from me. But through it all, I held onto the hope that we were meant to be a family, and that somehow, we would make it through.

5. Build Your Support System

Adoption is not something you do alone. It takes a village, and building a strong support system is crucial. Surround yourself with people who understand the challenges of adoption—whether it's family, friends, or support groups for adoptive parents. These people will be your lifeline during the tough moments and your cheerleaders during the celebrations.

Adoption Process Checklist

• Research: Understand the different types of adoption and choose the right path for your family.

• Choose an Agency or Attorney: If you're pursuing private or international adoption, select a reputable agency or attorney to guide you through the process.

• Attend Adoption Information Sessions: Many agencies offer information sessions to help you understand what to expect during the process.

• Complete the Application: This is the first formal step in the adoption process, where you'll submit paperwork to begin your adoption journey.

• Home Study: Prepare for an in-depth assessment of your home and your ability to provide for a child.

• Background Checks: Expect to undergo criminal background checks, fingerprinting, and medical evaluations as part of the process.

• Parenting Classes: Some adoptions, especially those through foster care, may require you to attend parenting classes.

• Matching Process: If adopting through foster care or private adoption, be prepared for the emotional process of being matched with a child. This can take time, so patience is key.

• Meet the Child: Depending on the type of adoption, you may have the opportunity to meet the child before the adoption is finalized.

- Finalization: Once the legal process is complete, celebrate the official finalization of your adoption in court.

Made in the USA
Columbia, SC
09 February 2025

53298313R00138